"You have my blessing. It's a book that needed to be written. It will do a lot of good".

Dr. Peter John Kreeft
Professor of Philosophy, Boston College

"Spirituality can seem like an amorphous, impractical, and un-Presbyterian pursuit. But historically nothing could be farther from the truth. For anyone seeking to explore the 'how's' of the Christian life, Stephen Hiemstra has provided a helpful, accessible guide using the classic catechetical structure of the Ten Commandments (how Christians should live), the Lord's Prayer (how Christians should pray), and the Apostles' Creed (how Christians should believe)".

Rev. David A. Currie, Ph.D.
Director of the Doctor of Ministry Program and
Associate Professor of Pastoral Theology, Gordon-Conwell Theological Seminary"

"With the rule of faith—Apostles Creed, 10 Commandments and Lord's Prayer—as his backdrop, Hiemstra opens up the subject of Christian spirituality with theological acumen and practical application. This is a book for those who want to understand how best to have a living faith and an ever deepening devotional and experiential knowledge of God."

Dr. Stephen Macchia
Founder and president of Leadership Transformations and director of the Pierce Center for Disciple-Building at Gordon-Conwell Theological Seminary.
Author of several books, most notably Becoming A Healthy Church (Baker) and Crafting A Rule of Life (InterVarsity/Formatio).

A CHRISTIAN GUIDE TO
SPIRITUALITY

Forgotten Path in Winter

A CHRISTIAN GUIDE TO SPIRITUALITY

Foundations for Disciples

Stephen W. Hiemstra

T2P

T2Pneuma Publishers LLC
Centreville, Virginia

A CHRISTIAN GUIDE TO SPIRITUALITY
Foundations for Disciples

T2Pneuma Publishers LLC
P.O. Box 230564, Centreville, Virginia 20120
www.T2Pneuma.com

ISBN–10: 0615971350
ISBN–13: 978–0–615–97135–3

Library of Congress Control Number: 2014933538

Printed by CreateSpace, An Amazon.com Company
Manufactured in the United States of America

All Scripture quotations, unless otherwise indicated, are taken from *The Holy Bible*, English Standard Version, Copyright © 2000; 2001 by Crossway Bibles, a division of Good News Publishers. Used by permission. All rights reserved.

Grateful acknowledgment is made for permission to use the following materials:

Office of the General Assembly, Presbyterian Church (U.S.A.); *Book of Confessions, Part I.* Used by permission.

Reprinted with permission from *The Heidelberg Catechism 450th Anniversary Edition* © Faith Alive Christian Resources, October 2013

The image on the front cover is a 12th century mosaic known as the *Hagia Sophia* (Holy Wisdom) from a basilica of the same name in Istanbul, Turkey. The electronic image is licensed from iStockPhoto (www.iStockPhoto.com) of Calgary in Alberta, Canada.

Cover design and photographs by SWH

To my wife, Maryam, and to our children, Christine, Narsis, and Reza, who inspired me to attend seminary and to write this book.

FORWARD

By Neal D. Presa[1]

*I*n 1991, the late Howard Rice, one of my distinguished, moderatorial predecessors, wrote a groundbreaking volume titled: *Reformed Spirituality: An Introduction for Believers.* He was one of the pioneers in the Presbyterian Church and at San Francisco Theological Seminary, where he taught in the emerging academic fields of spiritual direction and spiritual formation. His volume was ground-breaking, as Morton Kelsey wrote in his own Foreword to the book: *"Rice has opened the door to a long-neglected treasury of Reformed spiritual practice."*

In the Reformed tradition we are often associated with systematic theologies, dogmatics, and distinctive worship styles and liturgical theologies. But speak of spirituality, and you will receive stares. One can think of Roman Catholic expressions of spirituality (such as Ignatian), Eastern Orthodox, patristic theologies, or Methodist pietism; but within the panoply of the

1 Middlesex, NJ, February 14, 2014. @NealPresa. Rev. Neal D. Presa, Ph.D. was Moderator of the 220th General Assembly of the Presbyterian Church (U.S.A.) from 2012–2014 and was chair of the General Assembly Special Committee on the Heidelberg Catechism from 2010–2012. He is associate pastor of the Village Community Presbyterian Church in Rancho Santa Fe, CA, and a distance faculty member as Extraordinary Associate Professor of Practical Theology of the North-West University in Potchestroom, South Africa. He previously served as a solo pastor in Middlesex, NJ and on the faculty of New Brunswick Theological Seminary, where he taught preaching, worship, and Presbyterian studies.

Christian household, let alone Protestantism specifically, the Reformed tradition has neglected this part of our DNA.

Yet, our 16th century Reformation forbears emphasized the work of the Holy Spirit and the Spirit's relationship to the Christian life and our lifelong discipleship of Jesus Christ. Both John Calvin and Martin Bucer wrote extensively on the person and work of the Holy Spirit and the ministry of Katharina Zell in Strasbourg with her husband Martin, and her own perspective on the Holy Spirit. In our own day, the insightful *Participation in Christ: An Entry into Karl Barth's Church Dogmatics* by Adam Neder (2009) and *Calvin, Participation and the Gift: The Activity of Believers in Union with Christ* by J. Todd Billings (2009) demonstrate the active interest and wide receptivity of the Church in engaging more deeply and fully Christian spirituality, our connection to the triune God through and in the Holy Spirit, and what that all means for our communal life and our faith in Jesus Christ.

We cannot have it any other way. To be a believer, to be a disciple of Jesus Christ, as sealed in our baptisms and whenever we gather at the Eucharistic Table, is to belong to the community of the triune God—both the community of the Trinity and the community of people that the Trinity has created, redeemed, and presently calls to bear witness of the Good News.

Jesus Christ spoke of the ongoing ministry of the Holy Spirit as: *"But the Advocate, the Holy Spirit, whom the Father will send in my name, will teach you everything, and remind you of all that I have said to you."* (John 14:26, NRSV)

We are anchored to the heart and life of the triune God, united to the ascended Christ, connected inextricably to the communion of saints in all times and in all places because of the Holy Spirit. We in the Reformed traditions neglect the person and work of the Holy Spirit at our peril. It is the Holy Spirit in whom, by whom, and through whom the duality of certainty and mystery are intertwined: the certainty of the sure promises of God in Christ and Christ's teachings; and the mystery of the when and where and how of following. Thus, the Holy Spirit mediates both the present absence of Christ and the present presence of Christ. We can, therefore, confess simultaneously without contradiction: Christ is fully absent from us as He is ascended, and Christ is fully present with us. Who enables us to live confidently, with faith, hope, and love, in that tension of certainty-mystery, absence-presence, is the Holy Spirit. And what the Holy Spirit does on this side of eternity is to apprentice our lives to the way of God the Father as revealed in Jesus

Christ.

That has been the journey of all believers, of all disciples of Jesus Christ—to have hearts that pulse after God's own, to have the mind of Christ, and to do the will of the Father. The ancient mystics sought it; the prophets declared it; monastic communities embodied it. We in the Reformed tradition don't customarily use prayer beads, incense, icons, and altars, although there has been a surge of Pottery Barn-style candles, the use of prayer labyrinths, and a desire to fully engage all of our senses in worship, or recapture what Hans Urs von Balthasar aptly described as theological aesthetics, beauty.

For ages, believers, communities of Christ's disciples saw in the the Apostles' Creed, the Lord's Prayer, and the Ten Commandments unique and distinct gifts from God for the people of God. These three sources commonly called the "rule of faith" (regula fidei) were utilized for nearly two millennia as a means to apprentice the faith.

The Creed provided a brief summary of the Gospel. The Gospel was, at its core and circumference, that which the Creed spoke about; or that whom the Creed describes: namely the Triune God. The Gospel is the Triune God Himself. God reveals; God gives. The reality that we as human beings are recipients of God's self-revelation and self-giving, that is great news! The Creed, referred to in many ancient liturgies and church manuals, became the document for baptismal preparation. Those who were to join the body of Christ would be taught the Creed, would commit it to memory, and would demonstrate that the Creed was fully metabolized in their hearts and minds by reciting it in the presence of the bishop, elders, and deacons.

The Lord's Prayer is apprenticeship language. Praying "Our Father..." was to kneel down next to our brother, our Lord, our Savior, who, likewise, prays that prayer. The Lord's Prayer is learning the language of the Holy Son, who desires to commune with our heavenly Father.

The Ten Commandments expressed the ethics of the community of disciples. In it are contained the exhortations to and prohibitions for the holy community to be the distinctive people of almighty God. It was law and ordinance, but it was also Good News because the Commandments emanated from the heart and life of God. God is truthful; God does not bear false witness; God does not kill; God is holy; God does not covet unholy things. To be recipients of the Ten Commandments, to practice it, to live it, to write it on our foreheads and doorposts was to be marked by God.

Each one of the components of the "rule of faith"— the Creed, the Lord's Prayer, and the Ten Commandments—and all of them together, shape and form and anchor us as disciples precisely and only because of the Holy Spirit. It is the Holy Spirit who writes upon our hearts and renews our minds. It is the Holy Spirit who unites us so fully to the living Lord and to one another, making possible and real that mysterious but real communion.

Stephen W. Hiemstra in *A Christian Guide to Spirituality: Foundations for Disciples* gives us in the Reformed traditions and the Church ecumenical a usable and user-friendly guide that is devotional, pastoral, educational, and deeply theological. Combining Scripture, anecdotal reflections, study questions, and prayer—he framed the book with the Creed, the Lord's Prayer, and the Decalogue as the infrastructure. Any book that invites and deepens our discipleship of the triune God through the "rule of faith" is always a good thing. What this book does that I very much appreciate is that it presents the Gospel again and again. The Gospel is the very fountain and foundation of our faith; because in it and through it, it is encountering the living God again and again.

PREFACE

Spirituality is lived belief. When we pray, worship, or reach out to our neighbors, we live out our beliefs. Our beliefs structure our spirituality like skin stretched over the bones of our bodies. These beliefs start with faith in God the Father through Jesus Christ as revealed through the Holy Spirit in scripture, the church, and daily life. Our theology orders our beliefs. Without a coherent theology, we lose our identity in space and time having no map or compass to guide us on our way. In the end, we focus on ourselves, not God.

Christian spirituality accordingly starts with God, not with us. Like the woman Jesus cured of a spinal disfiguration, our only response can be to glorify God with songs of praise (Luke 13:13). This is why lasting Christian joy is experienced, not with recognizing Christ as savior, but with recognizing Christ as Lord. Spiritual disciplines and experiences are part of this spirituality, but they are not necessarily the focus (1 Cor 13:8).

This focus on what God has done begins in verse one of Genesis where God is pictured creating the heavens and the earth. What exactly have we done to deserve being created? Nothing. In fact, our first independent act was to sin. What exactly have we done to warrant forgiveness? Nothing. Christ died for our sins. The only meaningful response to these gifts of creation and salvation is praise.

The early church interpreted and summarized God's revelations in the biblical text and early creeds. The catechisms were developed later to summarize key church doctrines. The Heidelberg Catechism, Luther's catechism, and the Catholic catechism focus on three key statements of faith: the Apostle's Creed, the Lord's Prayer, and the Ten Commandments (Chan 2006, 108). Not surprisingly, Sunday morning worship has for centuries focused on these three faith statements, often being memorized and put to music. The Heidelberg Catechism, for example, encourages a focus on worship and is itself divided into 52 sermon topics for weekly use.

The key spiritual discipline in the Christian faith naturally is Sunday morning worship. The worship service includes prayer, readings from scripture, the spoken word, the sacraments, music, statements of faith, and other expressions of faithful worship. In worship, music binds our hearts and minds.

This worship experience is strengthened daily through devotions; those personal, as well as with our spouses, families, and other small groups. The original small group is the Trinity—Father, Son, and Holy Spirit—our template for healthy community. And when we take our spirituality into the work world, it too becomes an opportunity for worship.

The pages that follow discuss Christian spirituality in the form of daily devotions. Each topic is treated with a scriptural reference, reflection, prayer, and questions for discussion. When appropriate, references are provided for further study. The first four chapters (Introduction, Apostle's Creed, Lord's Prayer, and Ten Commandments) cover 40 days, making them suitable as a Lenten study. The entire study is 50 days, consistent with beginning a study on Easter and running through Pentecost.

My prayer is that this book will encourage readers both to understand Christian spirituality better and to nurture their walk with the Lord. There is no such thing as quality time with the Lord; there is only time. The living God speaks to us in many ways, but especially through scripture, and, having initiated a dialog, expects our response (Thielicke 1962, 34).

ACKNOWLEDGMENTS

*A*s Christians and as pastors, we are nurtured by many saints in ways that can sometimes be hard to enumerate. After a point, however, we come to realize that the Holy Spirit is the true author of the illumination and the inspiration of the work that we call ours. This study has truly been a blessing to me.

November 15, 2013 marked the 450th anniversary of the publishing of the Heidelberg Catechism. While some have described this book as a devotional commentary on the Heidelberg Catechism, it is more correct to say that the book and the catechism share a common focus on the Apostle's Creed, the Lord's Prayer, and the Ten Commandments. The catechism was helpful, however, in developing these reflections. Special thanks to the Reformed Church in America for making the scriptural references to the Heidelberg Catechism available on its website[1].

I want to thank all of my reviewers. Special thanks to go to Rev. Dr. John E. Hiemstra of the Reformed Church in America, to Rev. Thomas J. Smith with I.T.E.M. Inc., to Nohemi Zerbi of Riverside Presbyterian Church, Sterling, VA, and to Rev. Sindile Dlamini, Chaplain: Howard University Hospital and

---

1 (FACR 2013).

Minister: Michigan Park Christian Ministries Washington DC.

Special thanks also to Reid Satterfield who has been my mentor and editor[2]. Reid is the former coordinator of the Pierce Center for Disciple Building at Gordon-Conwell Theological Seminary in Charlotte, NC and in that role he recruited me into the fellowship. The Pierce Fellowship became my home away from home in seminary and helped develop my passion for discipling and spiritual development which matured into this book.

Finally, I would like to acknowledge Lynne K. Zusman, my attorney, for her helpful business advice, legal counsel, and constant encouragement.

---

2 Reid was a missionary for African Inland Mission and currently serves as the Coordinator of Discipleship and Spiritual Formation at St. Patrick's Anglican Mission, Charlotte, NC. He also lecturers for Perspectives that provides churches with educational resources for engaging in world missions and provide spiritual direction to church leaders in and around the Charlotte Metro area.

CONTENTS

THE LORD'S PRAYER

THE TEN COMMANDMENTS

SPIRITUAL DISCIPLINES

CONCLUSIONS

INTRODUCTION

WHY IS SPIRITUALITY IMPORTANT?

WHO IS GOD?

WHO ARE WE?

WHAT SHOULD WE DO?

HOW DO WE KNOW?

Spirituality is lived belief[1]. Even if we are not always fully aware of it, each of us has a theology we practice. When we insist on doing things our own way, for example, we deny God's sovereignty over that portion of our life[2], creating a blind spot. If circumstances later force us to rethink what we have done, then we may find ourselves living out a theology we would not choose given more time to reflect.

A helpful framework for reflecting on our personal theology comes in the form of four questions taken from philosophy[3]. These questions are:

1. Who is God? (metaphysics);

2. Who are we? (anthropology);

3. What should we do? (ethics); and

4. How do we know? (epistemology).

In the beginning our devotions we will focus on these questions and then return to them, from time to time, to see what we can learn.

---

1 Simon Chan (1998, 16) writes: *"spirituality refers to a kind of life that is formed by a particular type of spiritual theology. Spirituality is a lived reality . . ."*

2 *"So then he has mercy on whomever he wills, and he hardens whomever he wills." (Rom 9:18)*

3 Peter Kreeft (2007, 6).

DAY 1: *Why is spirituality important?*

"Jesus said to him, 'I am the way, and the truth, and the life. No one comes to the Father except through me.'" (John 14:6)

S ome questions defy pat answers: Who is God? Who am I? What must I do? How do I know?

At one point in world competition among marathon runners, Ethiopians ruled. The Kenyans had talent, but Ethiopians trained harder and trained better. Training at high altitudes built their strength; training as a team built their competitiveness.

Africans were not always allowed to compete in these games. The right to compete did not come all at once, but it started with efforts to abolish slavery. William Wilberforce, a devout Christian, spent most of his life leading the effort to abolish slavery in nineteenth century Great Britain. He later wrote about the need for spiritual training saying:

> *no one expects to attain the height of learning, or arts, or power, or wealth, or military glory, without vigorous resolution, and strenuous diligence, and steady perseverance. Yet we expect to be Christians without labor,*

study, or inquiry. (Wilberforce 2006, 5–6)

Wilberforce must have had me in mind. For years, I professed Christ as savior, but did not embrace him as Lord. My faith was incomplete. As I learned to apply the lordship of Christ to my life, I experienced a more sustained sense of Christian joy.

The content of faith is critical. *"Now faith is the assurance of things hoped for, the conviction of things not seen."* (Heb 11:1) If I have faith that eggshells are white, I have only defined eggshell color. But, if I have faith that Christ rose from the dead, my whole world changes—God exists and death no longer has the final word. The call to faith defines our identity in Christ[1].

The idea of Christian faith has become unfashionable. The postmodern world we live in is often like the Sahara desert where mountains of sand blow about daily. Direction in a world of shifting sand requires a surveyor's marker that establishes location. Standing on a marker, a map shows both direction and distance. Without the marker, however, a map becomes a puzzle—like words without definitions—whose pieces have meaning only relative to one another. Scripture is our map; our

---

1 *"Through the CALL of Jesus men become individuals. Whilly-nilly, they are compelled to decide, and that decision can only be made by themselves."* (Bonhoeffer 1995, 94).

marker is Jesus Christ[2].

The sun does not always shine; neither does it rain every day. Spirituality is living out what we know to be true on good days and *bad*.

Almighty Father: thank you for the person of Jesus of Nazareth; who lived as a role model for sinners; who died as a ransom for sin; and whose resurrection gives us the hope of salvation. In the power of your Holy Spirit, inspire the words written and illumine the words read. In Jesus' name. Amen.

Questions

1.   What led you to study this book?

2.   How are physical and spiritual training similar?

3.   Who was William Wilberforce and why do we remember him?

4.   What is faith? Why does it matter what we believe?

5.   What uncertainties do you experience in life?

6.   Why is scripture like a map? How is Jesus like a marker?

---

2 Benner (2002, 26) sees the role of a spiritual director as of pointing to God's work in a person's life.

DAY 2: Who is God?

The heavens declare the glory of God, and the sky above proclaims his handiwork. Day to day pours out speech, and night to night reveals knowledge. There is no speech, nor are there words, whose voice is not heard. (Ps 19:1–3)

When I was young, I wanted to be a pilot. I learned to read a map, work with a compass, and navigate by the stars in pursuit of my goal. The idea that God would use a star to guide the wise men to the baby Jesus fascinated me. Equally fascinating is how God reveals himself to us in the creation story. The Bible starts telling us that: *"In the beginning, God created the heavens and the earth."* (Gen 1:1) What do these simple words tell us about God?

The phrase—in the beginning—tells us that God is eternal. If creation has a beginning, then it must also have an end. This implies that creation is not eternal, but the God who created it must be. If our eternal God created time, both the beginning and the end, then everything God created belongs to God. Just as the potter is master over the pottery he makes, God is sovereign over creation (Jer 18:4–8). God did not win creation in an arm-wrestling match or buy it online or find it on the street, he created it—God is a worker[1].

God's sovereignty is reinforced in the second half of the sentence when it says: God created the heavens and the earth. Here heaven and earth form a poetic construction called a merism. A merism is a literary device that can be compared to defining a line segment by referring to its end points. The expression—heaven and earth—therefore means that God created everything[2]. Because he created everything, he is sovereign over creation; and sovereignty implies ownership[3].

So, from the first sentence in the Bible we know that God is eternal and he is sovereign. We also know that he is holy. Why? Are heaven and earth equal? No. Heaven is God's residence. From the story of Moses' encounter with God in the burning bush (Exod 3:5), we learn that any place where God is becomes holy in the sense of being set apart or sacred. Because God resides in heaven, it must be holy. Earth is not. Still, God created both and is sovereign over both (Rev 4:11).

Genesis paints two other important pictures of God.

The first picture arises in Genesis 1:2; here the breath, or

---

1 Hugh Whelchel (2012,7).

2 Heaven and earth can also be interpreted as proxies for God's attributes of transcendence and immanence (Jer 23:23-24; Dyck 2014, 99).

3 God's eternal nature is also defined with a merism: *"I am the Alpha and the Omega,"* says the Lord God, *"who is and who was and who is to come, the Almighty."* (Rev 1:8)

spirit of God, is pictured like a bird hovering over the waters[1]. Hovering requires time and effort suggesting ongoing participation in and care for creation. The Bible speaks exhaustively about God providing for us—God's provision. Breath translates as Holy Spirit in the original languages of the Bible—both Hebrew (Old Testament) and Greek (New Testament)[2].

The second picture appears in Genesis 2, which retells the story of creation in more personal terms. As a potter works with clay (Isa 64:8), God forms Adam and puts him in a garden. Then, he talks to Adam and directs him to give the animals names. And when Adam gets lonely, God creates Eve from Adam's rib or side—a place close to his heart.

Genesis 1 and 2, accordingly, paint three pictures of God: 1. God as a mighty creator; 2. God who meticulously attends to his creation; and 3. God who walks with us like a friend. While the Trinity is not fully articulated in scripture until the New Testament, God's self-disclosure as the Trinity appears from the beginning (Chan 1998, 41).

The Lord's Prayer casts a new perspective on Genesis

---

1 This bird (avian) image appears again in the baptismal accounts of Jesus. For example, in Matthew 3:16 we read: *"And when Jesus was baptized, immediately he went up from the water, and behold, the heavens were opened to him, and he saw the Spirit of God descending like a dove and coming to rest on him."*

2Breath itself is necessary for life—part of God's provision.

1:1 when Jesus says: *"Your kingdom come, your will be done, on earth as it is in heaven."* (Matt 6:10) Because we are created in God's image, we want our home to modeled after God's.

Heavenly Father: We praise you for creating heaven and earth; for creating all that is, that was, and that is to come; for creating things seen and unseen. We praise you for sharing yourself in the person of Jesus of Nazareth; our role model in life, redeemer in death, and hope for the future. We praise you for the Holy Spirit, who is present with us showering us with spiritual gifts and sustaining all things. Open our hearts; illumine our minds; strengthen our hands in your service. In Jesus' name, Amen.

Questions

1. What part of the creation story is most meaningful to you?

2. How is merism helpful in understanding God's nature? How does it differ from image?

3. How does God relate to time? How do we know?

4. What is special about heaven? How do we know?

5. What are God's attributes? What do holy, eternal, and sovereign mean?

DAY 3: *Who are we?*

"Who do people say that I am?" And they told him, John the Baptist; and others say, Elijah; and others, one of the prophets." And he asked them, "But who do you say that I am?" Peter answered him, "You are the Christ." (Mark 8:27–29)

Who is Jesus Christ to you?

Jesus' question to the disciples—who do people say that I am—is a question that demands a response. Is Jesus a good teacher; a prophet; a savior; or Lord of Lords? Our response depends on our belief about Jesus' identity (Chan 1998, 40). It also informs us as to who we once were, who we are now, and who we will become in the future.

If Jesus is merely a good teacher, then our actions are motivated primarily by abstract obligation. We might as easily be guided by the Ten Commandments. Law has the virtue of being clear and concrete. The Ten Commandments outline moral law while other parts of the first five books of the Bible give us both ceremonial law (how to worship) and case law (what to do in special situations). However, the abstract nature of this obligation means that it is contingent on the commitment of the heart. The mind acknowledges the obligation, but the heart is uncommitted.

If Jesus is only a prophet, then our actions are motivated by abstract expectation. A focus on law is possible because the role of an Old Testament prophet was, primarily, to remind people of their obligation under the law. However, both head and heart are contingent—we do not know if the prophecy will take place or if we care. In short, we are conflicted and uncommitted.

If Jesus is only a savior, then our actions are motivated primarily by the act of receiving. We cherish the assurance of salvation, but never count the cost (Luke 14:27–30). In effect, we have become fans—long on enthusiasm, but short on commitment. Fans want entertainment and a good show—they want a winning team. The Apostle's Creed, the Lord's Prayer, and the Ten Commandments are all things that we have committed to memory, but when things become inconvenient our resolve dissipates.

If Jesus is Lord of lords, then our actions are motivated by an obligation of loyalty. In this case, our response is qualitatively different because both our hearts and minds are committed. We want to be just like Jesus. We want to act like Jesus; we want to pray like Jesus; we want to tell Jesus' life story. Suddenly, the Apostle's Creed, the Lord's Prayer, and the Ten Commandments start looking like important clues as to how to pray, to live our lives, and to discuss our faith with others.

Jesus is also the perfect match between form (being divine and human) and content (without sin). In the Hebrew mind, this perfect match makes Him both good and beautiful (Dyrness 2001, 81). Loyalty is a fitting characteristic for a servant and it a characteristic of Christ himself (Phil 2:5–11). Our loyalty to God accordingly allows us to share in Christ's goodness and his beauty—has anyone told you lately that you are beautiful? (Isa 62:5)

The church is composed of people who mostly share one thing in common—we are forgiven. Each of us must walk the path of faith alone, but at no step along the way are we truly alone because Jesus walks with us. If we persist in the walk of faith, our perception of Jesus will evolve from teacher to prophet to savior, and Lord of Lords. As we make this journey, our response to restoration and identity as persons will likewise evolve.

Almighty Father, beloved son, ever-present Spirit. We praise you for creating us in your image, for walking with us even as we sin, and for patiently restoring us into your favor. Strengthen our sense of your identity. In the power of your Holy Spirit, unstop our ears; uncover our eyes; soften our hearts; illumine our minds. Shape us more and more in your image that we also might grow. In Jesus' precious name, Amen.

Questions

1. Who is Jesus Christ to you?

2. What are the dominant images of Jesus that we see? How does our image of Jesus affect what we do?

3. What is the thing that everyone in the church shares in common?

4. How did your life change when you came to faith? What milestones have occurred since then? What hurdles are you dealing with now?

DAY 4: *What should we do?*

"So God created man in his own image, in the image of God he created him; male and female he created them." (Gen 1:27)

*H*ave you accepted Christ into all aspects of your life? Walking into an office, whose picture normally hangs on the wall? The picture on the wall usually depicts the one casting the vision of the company. It could be the founder, the current president, or a chief executive. Why? It is helpful to remind us who is in charge and what we are about.

Assume you are a new office manager. Suppose when your supervisor was out of the office, a stranger walked in and questioned your supervisor's instructions, saying—you are in charge now: take it easy. Then, being naive, you declared independence, kicked the feet up on the desk, and slept all afternoon. What would happen when your supervisor returned? What would you think then if the supervisor, even as you are being fired and walked to the door, made a promise—when my oldest son comes, you can come back and he will make sure that stranger does not bother you anymore?

This is essentially the story of Adam and Eve. The story has three parts: creation with great expectations (hired), fall into temptation (fired), and promise of restoration through divine intervention (second chance).

Creation. Just like the business with the picture on the wall, in our hearts we have a picture of God because God created us in his image. This family resemblance gives us human dignity. We were created with great prospects and a bright future.

The emphasis in Genesis 1:27 is on being created in the image of God together with our spouses. We were created to live in families with one man and one woman. To prevent any misunderstanding, Adam and Eve were blessed, put in charge on earth, and given a mission: *"Be fruitful and multiple."* (Gen 1:28)

Fall. God placed Adam and Eve in the Garden of Eve with just one restriction that came with a penalty: do not eat of the tree of the knowledge of good and evil under penalty of death (Gen 2:17). In deceiving Eve, Satan questioned God's integrity saying that the penalty was a lie: you will not die (Gen 3:4). In giving into this temptation, Adam and Even sinned and rebelled against God. God then expelled them from the Garden of Eden. Left outside Eden, Adam and Eve faced life outside of God's presence and the penalty of death.

Restoration. In God's curse of Satan, he prophesied the

coming of Christ. Satan's usurped kingdom will be over-thrown by a descendant of Eve (Gen 3:15).

What does the story of Adam and Eve say about our identity? Tension arises in our lives because we do not live up to God's expectations. Our dignity arises from being created in God's image; yet, we sin and rebel against God. The Good News is that when Christ died for our sins, he overthrew the rule of Satan in our lives and restored our relationship with God, just as it was in the beginning.

Eternal and Compassionate Father. Help us to accept You into all aspects of our lives. Thank you for creating us in your image. Bless our families. Forgive our sin and rebellion. In the power of your Holy Spirit, restore to us the joy of your salvation. In Jesus' name. Amen.

Questions

1. In your own words, explain the story of Adam and Eve

2. What are the three parts of the story?

3. Why is the story of Adam and Eve meaningful to us today?

4. What sins do you struggle with now?

DAY 5: *How do we know?*

All Scripture is breathed out by God and profitable for teaching,

for reproof, for correction, and for training in righteousness, that

the people of God may be complete, equipped for every good work.

(2 Tim 3:16–17)

*I*n the Koran, Christians are described as people of the book. Part of the reason for this distinction may be that the New Testament was the first text bound as a book. Books were cheaper to produce and more portable than scrolls, which continued to be used, for example, to record the Hebrew Bible. It is noteworthy that more New Testament texts have survived from ancient times than any other ancient manuscripts[1].

Athanasius suggested the twenty-seven books which now make up the New Testament in his Easter letter of AD 367 was later confirmed by the Council of Carthage in AD 397. The common denominator in these books is that their authors were known to have been an apostle or associated closely with an apostle of Jesus. Pope Damasus I commissioned Jerome to prepare an authoritative translation of the Bible into Latin in AD

1 The technical description is the Bible was the first publication to appear in widespread circulation as a codex (bound book) (Metzger and Ehrman 2005, 15). Stone (2010, 14) cites the existence of 5,500 partial or complete biblical manuscripts making it the only document from the ancient world with more than a few dozen copies.

382 commonly known as the Vulgate (Evans 2005, 162). The Vulgate remained the authoritative Biblical text for the church until the time of the Reformation when the reformers began translating the Bible into common languages.

During the reformation Martin Luther, for example, translated the New Testament into German in 1522 and followed with an Old Testament translation in 1532[1]. Luther kept the twenty-seven books of the New Testament, but followed the Masoretic (Hebrew Old Testament) rather than the Septuagint (Greek Old Testament) in selecting books for the Old Testament[2]. The books left out became known as the Apocrypha. These books continue to distinguish the Catholic (Apocrypha included) from Protestant Bible translations (Apocrypha excluded) to this day. The list given below, which excludes the Apocrypha, is taken from the Westminster Confession:

OLD TESTAMENT

Genesis, Exodus, Leviticus, Numbers, Deuteronomy, Joshua, Judges, Ruth, 1 Samuel, 2 Samuel, 1 Kings, 2 Kings, 1 Chronicles, 2 Chronicles, Ezra, Nehemiah, Esther, Job, Psalms, Prov-

---

[1]Luther completed the entire Bible in 1534 (Bainton 1995, 255).
[2]Luther translated the Apocrpha in 1534 but specifically said they were not canonical, just good to read (see: http://www.lstc.edu/gruber/luthers_bible/1534.php).

erbs, Ecclesiastes, Song of Solomon, Isaiah, Jeremiah, Lamentations, Ezekiel, Daniel, Hosea, Joel, Amos, Obadiah, Jonah, Micah, Nahum, Habakkuk, Zephaniah, Haggai, Zechariah, Malachi

NEW TESTAMENT

Matthew, Mark, Luke, John, Acts, Romans, 1 Corinthians, 2 Corinthians, Galatians, Ephesians, Colossians, Philippians, 1 Thessalonians, 2 Thessalonians, 1 Timothy, 2 Timothy, Titus, Philemon, Hebrews, James, 1 Peter, 2 Peter, 1 John, 2 John, 3 John, Jude, Revelation

In our study of the Bible, Jesus' attitude about scripture guides our thinking. Jesus said:

> *Do not think that I have come to abolish the Law or the Prophets; I have not come to abolish them but to fulfill them. For truly, I say to you, until heaven and earth pass away, not an iota, not a dot, will pass from the Law until all is accomplished (Matt 5:17–18).*

The Law of Moses refers to the Law (first five books of the Bible) and the Prophets (the other books).

The last book in the Old Testament to be written was

likely Malachi which was written about four hundred years before the birth of Christ. The last book in the New Testament to be written was likely the book of Revelation which was written around 90 AD.

The Bible represents the work of many authors, yet its contents are uniquely consistent. This consistency adds weight to our belief that the Bible was inspired by the Holy Spirit.

Heavenly Father, breathe on us your breath of life. Soften our hearts to receive your word and bolster our minds to understand it. Restore to us the joy of your salvation. In Jesus' precious name. Amen.

Questions

1.   How old is the Bible?

2.   Why was the Bible assembled into a book?

3.   What rule was used to collect the books of the New Testament? How about the OT?

4.   What was Jesus' view of scripture?

5.   Why do we say that the Bible is inspired by the Holy Spirit?

THE APOSTLE'S CREED

I believe in God, the Father Almighty,

Creator of Heaven and Earth.

I believe in Jesus Christ, his only Begotten Son, our Lord,

who *was Conceived by the Holy Spirit*

and *Born of the Virgin Mary.*

He Suffered under Pontius Pilate,

was *Crucified, Died, and was Buried;*

He Descended to Hell. The Third Day He Rose again from the Dead.

He Ascended to Heaven and is Seated at the Right Hand of God the

Father Almighty.

From *there He will come to Judge the Living and the Dead.*

I believe in the Holy Spirit,

the *Holy Catholic Church,*

the *Communion of Saints,*

the *Forgiveness of Sins;*

the *Resurrection of the Body,*

and *the Life Everlasting. Amen*[1].

---

1 The references in this chapter to the Apostle's Creed are all taken from
FACR (2013, Q/A 23). Another translation is found in (PCUSA 1999,
2.1—2.3). No further footnoting of these references will be made in the titles
to individual devotions but they will be marked with this symbol (✿).

The Apostle's Creed is a statement faith focused on the question: WHO IS GOD? The answer given is that God is the Father, Son, and Holy Spirit who created the universe around us, lived among us, and dwells in us.

The Apostle's Creed also answers the other three philosophical questions:

- WHO ARE WE? We are disciples of Christ who sit at his feet to learn from him and follow his example.

- WHAT DO WE DO ABOUT IT? We believe in God and live out his plan for our lives. In this process, we learn about God's healthy boundaries for our lives.

- HOW DO WE KNOW? Individually and through the church, we relate directly with God and understand his will for our lives through scripture.

Unlike the Ten Commandments and the Lord's Prayer, the Apostle's Creed summarizes the story of Jesus, which the New Testament describes as the Gospel.

DAY 6: *What do you believe about God?*

But this is the covenant that I will make with the house of Israel after those days, declares the LORD: I will put my law within them, and I will write it on their hearts. And I will be their God, and they shall be my people. (Jer 31:33)

Once as a youth leader, I asked each member of the group to write out a personal statement of faith. This assignment kept us busy all evening. In the end, most kids had statements resembling the Apostle's Creed. For the Christian faith, this creed is foundational.

The Apostle's Creed began as a baptismal statement of faith in the fourth century (Rogers 1991, 61–62). It has evolved into a key statement of faith that is often memorized and proclaimed in worship services around the world.

The Apostle's Creed divides into three parts: Father, Son, and Holy Spirit. Each part helps us to understand and to indentify better to each person of the Trinity. The confession about the Father focuses on his role as creator. The confession about the Son recounts the story of Jesus Christ—conception, birth, death, resurrection, ascension, and return. The confession about the Holy Spirit links the Spirit to the work and key doctrines of the church.

The Apostle's Creed primarily tells the story of Jesus. Other parts of the creed appear simply to bracket the story of Jesus. This is not an accident. The four Gospel narratives each focus on the story of Jesus. Early church sermons, recorded in the Book of Acts, also often focus on telling Jesus' life story[1]. In general, the New Testament focuses on telling Jesus' life story and applying his story to our lives.

When is the last time that you shared Jesus' life story? How has Jesus' life become a model for your life?

Heavenly Father. We praise you for shepherding us and resting with us in lush gardens. Feed our hungering and thirsting souls as we confront sickness and death. Shelter us in your strong arms as we shelter the weak among us. Prosper us in righteousness as we model your love to those around us. Grant us your mercy through the storms of life until you lead us home (Ps 23). In the name of the Father, the Son, and the Holy Spirit, Amen.

Questions

1. If you wrote a statement of your faith, what elements

---

1 Sermons by both Peter (Acts 2:14–41; 10:34–43) and Paul (Acts13:16–41) focus on Jesus' life story.

should be included?

2.   What are the three parts to the Apostle's Creed? Which is
the longest?

3.   Find a sermon in Acts that recites the story of Jesus.

DAY 7: Almighty Creator

"I believe in God the Father Almighty, Maker of heaven and earth"⳨

od's humility expressed through the incarnation in Jesus Christ shines a light on His sovereignty (Matt 21:5)[1]. Truly powerful people can be fearlessly humble—they have nothing to prove and no one dares to challenge their authority. Their inherent strength and self-confidence makes them easy to work for[2]. By analogy, an almighty God is generous and can be approached easily. Why should we be any different?

When King David wrote—*"The heavens declare the glory of God, and the sky above proclaims his handiwork" (Ps 19:1)*, he did not just have creation's beauty in mind. The order of the universe points to the glory and sovereignty of God. Everywhere that scientists have studied, the same laws of physics apply. Why should there only be one set of physical laws?

As David implies, the order and stability of the created universe testifies to God's existence and sovereignty. Kurt Gödel, a Czech mathematician, who was born in 1906, educated in Vienna, and taught at Princeton University. He is famous

1 The Apostle Paul writes: *"when I am weak, then I am strong" (2 Cor 12:10).*
2 By contrast, the second and third tier managers often compete for more authority and always have their knives out.

for his incompleteness theorem published in 1931. This theorem states that stability in any closed, logical system requires that at least one assumption be taken from outside that system[3]. If creation is a closed, logical system (having only one set of physical laws suggests that it is) and exhibits stability, then it too must contain at least one external assumption. God, himself, fulfills that assumption (Smith 2001, 89).

God's sovereignty anchors His goodness. Three reasons can be cited. First, because God's authority flows out of His creative work (not through coercion, deception, or random events), it is legitimate (Jer 18:4). Legitimate authority is inherently good[4]. Second, God's authority as law-maker implies that if God says creation is good, then it is—by fiat—good (Gen 1:10). Third, in a practical sense, God's sovereignty reduces uncertainty; and stability is good[5].

As sons and daughters of God, we are to take comfort in

---

3 An example can be seen in economics as applied to price theory. The U.S. economy requires one price be set outside the economy (in the world market) to assure stability. In the nineteenth century, that price was gold, and the system was called the gold standard. Every price in the U.S. economy could be expressed in terms of how much gold it was worth. Now, the dollar functions that way.

4 Turning this statement around—we exist only because of God's goodness and existance is good. The authority that made this happen must also be good.

5Adam and Eve's sin in the garden was an act of rebellion and destroyed this aspect of stability.

His sovereignty because, as heirs to His kingdom, His image is also our image (Gen 1:27). Therefore, we can be confident in our ability to deal with life's challenges because God is for us and with us (Rom 8:28). What greater blessing could there be?

Almighty God. We praise you for creating the heavens and the earth; creating all that is, was, or will ever be; and creating things seen and unseen. We look on the order and beauty of your creation and break forth singing your praises. Grant us strength for each new day to reflect your goodness in joyful praise to those around us. In the name of the Father, the Son, and the Holy Spirit, Amen.

Questions

1. Why is humility a sign of God's sovereignty?

2. How does the order of the universe point to God's existence and sovereignty?

3. If God were weak, how would it affect His goodness?

4. How does God's authority and power directly benefit us? Why?

DAY 8: *Jesus Christ*

"I believe in Jesus Christ, his only begotten Son, our Lord."✝

N ames often tell a story. The name, Jesus Christ, is no
exception.

When we use the name, Jesus, in English, we are trans-
literating the Greek of the New Testament. Jesus' given name
was actually Joshua which means "he saves" in Hebrew. However, because Greek does not have an "SH" sound, Joshua could
not be accurately transliterated in New Testament Greek. Consequently, we borrowed Jesus from the Greek.

Joshua's role in the Old Testament is instructive. Moses
commissioned Joshua to lead the nation of Israel with these
words:

> *And the Lord commissioned Joshua the son of Nun and*
> *said, "Be strong and courageous, for you shall bring the*
> *people of Israel into the land that I swore to give them. I*
> *will be with you." (Deut 31:23)[1]*

Jesus' given name, Joshua, summarizes his commission.
However, Jesus' salvation arises as he brings us, not into the
Promised Land, but into Heaven (Heb 4:1–11). This salvation,

---

1 Because of Moses' sin at Meribah, God forbad Moses from bringing the
people of Israel into the Promised Land himself (Num 20:8–12).

furthermore, arises not from law, but from grace (Phil 3:2–11).

When we use the name, Jesus Christ, Christ is not Jesus' last name. Christ translates the Hebrew word, Messiah, into Greek and it means *anointed one* because during the commissioning process oil was poured on your head. Priests, prophets, and kings were anointed. The New Testament pictures Jesus fulfilling the roles of each of these three types of messiahs.

Jesus' messianic role is highlighted in the Book of Hebrews where we read:

> So *also Christ did not exalt himself to be made a high priest, but was appointed by him who said to him, "You are my Son, today I have begotten you"; as he says also in another place, "You are a priest forever, after the order of Melchizedek." (Heb 5:5–6)*

Melchizedek was the king of Salem (later called Jerusalem) and he was also a priest (Gen 14:18)[1]. Saying that Jesus is a priest of the order of Melchizedek expresses the idea that he is also a king. In Matt 24:1–2 Jesus prophesied the destruction of the temple in Jerusalem, which occurred later in AD 70, con-

---

1 In Hebrew Melchizedek means righteous king and some believe it to have been a title given to Shem, the righteous son of Noah (Gen 9:28). Ps 110, which is quoted in Heb 5:6, also associated King David with Melchizedek.

firming his prophetic role.

When we confess that Jesus is the only son of God[2], we acknowledge Jesus' divinity and exclusively as savior (John 3:16–17). God's infinite nature poses a problem for us because we are finite. Only someone divine can cross the divide between the infinite and the finite. In Jesus Christ, God crosses the divide to initiate the conversation and mediate for us—an act of grace—as high priest (Heb 5:1)[3].

Heavenly God. We praise you for graciously sending your son, our Lord and Savior, Jesus Christ. We give glory to his name— our perfect priest, prophet, and king. In the power of your Holy Spirit, help us also to listen to his voice and obey his commands. In Jesus' name, Amen.

Questions

1.   Where does the name, Jesus, come from? What does it mean?

---

2 Son of God is also, of course, a kingly title closely related to the title that Jesus preferred to call himself—son of man—which immediately brings to mind the prophesy of Dan 7.

3 The parable of the tenants highlights the exclusively of Jesus' role as mediator (Matt 21:33–40). The parable of the wedding feast addresses the problem created when we reject Jesus as mediator (Matt 22:2–14). When we confess Jesus as God's one and only son, we acknowledge God's sovereignty in determining the means of our salvation.

2.   What does Christ mean? What are the three types of messiah?

3.   Who is Melchizedek and why is he special?

4.   Why is communication with God difficult? Why is Christ's
mediating role exclusive?

DAY 9: *Immaculate Conception*[1]

"who was conceived by the Holy Spirit and born of the virgin Mary."✝

D o you ever feel isolated from God?

This isolation is not an accident. In the absence of Christ, two gaps exist between God and humanity: a gap in being (infinite versus finite) and a gap in holiness[2]. The Immaculate Conception of Mary allows Jesus to bridge both gaps (Matt 1:18ff).

The first gap requires that a mediator be both divine and human. In bridging the first gap, the Immaculate Conception introduces the divinity of Christ before his birth. He is then born by the usual means. Jesus could then serve as a bridge between an infinite God and finite humanity[3]. As the angel told Mary: *"nothing will be impossible with God." (Luke 1:37)*

The second gap requires that any mediator between humanity and God be without sin—holy. Jesus also bridges the second gap by living a sinless life. This work starts when Mary

---

1 The term, Immaculate Conception, is the idea that Jesus was born without the intervention of a human father. Accordingly, Mary remained a virgin.

2 The need for an intermediary is first articulated by the prophet Job: *"For I know that my Redeemer lives, and at the last he will stand upon the earth." (Job 19:25)*

3 Heb 2:14, 17.

assents to the angel's request (Luke 1:38) and continues through Jesus' lifelong work of teaching, healing, and reflecting God. Jesus' work ended on the cross when he declared: *"It is finished."* (John 19:30)

Jesus' birth follows the promise-fulfilment motif in the Old Testament record. The prophecy—*"Behold, the virgin shall conceive and bear a son, and shall call his name Immanuel"* *(Isa 7:14)*—reminds us of several miraculous pregnancies. The pattern of prophecy and pregnancy (e.g. promise-fulfillment) occurs again in births of Isaac (Gen 17:17), Jacob[1], the prophet Samuel and of John the Baptist[2]. However, in the case of Jesus, the role of prophecy was amplified.

For example, in the case of Isaac, both the timing and means (miraculous pregnancy) were prophesied. For Jesus, the instrumentality (virgin birth—Isa 7:14), his character (Isa 9:6), covenantal role[3], the place of birth (Bethlehem—Mic 5:2), and his lineage (House of David—2 Sam 7:12–16) were all prophesied. The elaborate birth narratives of Matthew and Luke testify to the reality of the humble nature of Jesus' birth. The prophe-

---

1 Gen 21:1–3, 25:21.
2 1 Sam 1:20; Luke 1:5–25.
3 Deut 18:18; Jer 31:33.

cies point to his divine nature.

The Immaculate Conception also reminds us of the absolute and creative sovereignty of God. When God creates the heaven and the earth, he creates them ex nihilo—out of nothing (Gen 1:1)[4]. The idea that Jesus is conceived ex-nihilo (without a biological father) at birth and then resurrected after death expresses God's absolute and creative sovereignty. It also suggests that, through Jesus Christ, God remains actively present in our lives too. This is very good news!

God of all wonders. We praise you for Mary's faithfulness and Jesus' miraculous birth. Bridge the gaps of holiness, time, and space between us. Open our minds to the miracles that we experience daily but neglect to think about. Open our hearts to accept your will for our lives. In the name of the Father, the Son, and the Holy Spirit, Amen.

Questions

1.   What two gaps did Jesus cross that we cannot cross for ourselves?

2.   What miracle births do we read about in scripture?

3.   What is the role of prophecy in Jesus's birth?

4 For example: Sproul 2003, 111.

DAY 10: Suffering

"He suffered under Pontius Pilate, was crucified, died, and was buried."✝

W hy do we care about Christ's suffering on the cross? The Apostle Peter said it best: *"By his wounds you have been healed". (1 Pet 2:24)*[1] The Jewish authorities said that Jesus claimed to be a king and charged Jesus with sedition (Mark 15:2)[2]. In fact, Jesus was a king (messiah) in the Jewish sense, but not a king (political rival) in a Roman sense. For this reason, the Roman Governor Pontius Pilate cross examined Jesus publicly and concluded: *"I find no guilt in him." (John 19:4)*

Jesus' link to Pontius Pilate underscores the credibility of his innocent suffering because, even by Roman standards, Pilate was corrupt and brutal—Pilate had Jesus both flogged and crucified solely to satisfy the blood lust of a crowd[3]. The link

---

1 The Apostle Paul likewise wrote: *"For while we were still weak, at the right time Christ died for the ungodly." (Rom 5:6)*

2 Crucifixion was a penalty for sedition—rebellion against the Roman state. The inscription that Pilate placed over Jesus on the cross in Latin read: *"Iesus Nazarenus rex Iudaeorum"* (John 19:19 VUL). It is usually recorded with the acronym, INRI, and translates as Jesus of Nazareth, King of the Jews.

3 By contrast, when the Apostle Paul found himself charged with profaning the temple only a few years later, another governor, Porcius Festus, simply kept him locked up for two years (Acts 24:6, 27). First century Jewish historian, Josephus (AD 38—100), records several accounts of Pilate that picture him as ruthlessness (Josephus 2009, 3.1).

to Pilate also links Jesus (and the Apostle's Creed) to a known, historical person. Not only is Pilate mentioned in Josephus, an inscription bearing the phrase *"Pontius Pilate Prefect of Judea"* was found in 1961 in the excavation of a theatre in Caesarea[4].

Jesus' death on the cross underscores his extreme suffering. The Romans devised crucifixion as a method of execution by torture—it amplified the suffering inflicted. It was a slow, painful death. Crucifixion was so horrific that Roman law forbade Roman citizens from being crucified.

In Jewish tradition, death on the cross meant that one was cursed by God[5]. This is what Paul meant when he wrote: *"Christ redeemed us from the curse of the law by becoming a curse for us— for it is written, cursed is everyone who is hanged on a tree." (Gal 3:13)*[6] The implication was that the crime committed was so horrible that the person deserved not only death but also eternal damnation. Burial behind a stone assured that Jesus was truly dead[7].

Because Jesus was sinless and remained innocent, even

---

4 Pilate was Roman prefect from 26 to 36 AD (Zondervan 2005, 1714).

5 Deut 21:22–23.

6 Also see: Acts 5:30, 10:39, and 13:29; 1 Pet 2:24.

7 The story of the death of Absalom illustrates this point. Absalom rebelled against his father, King David, and raised an army to over-throw him. When his hair got caught in a tree, he was considered cursed by God. David's commander, Joab, had Absalom publically executed, buried in a pit, and covered with stones (2 Sam 18:10–18).

in death, he became the only sinless person to live after Adam (Heb 4:15). Unlike Adam, Jesus, whose sinless life came to an abrupt end, never gave into temptation. In death, he was accordingly a perfect (without defeat or blemish) sin offering (Lev 4:22–24). In doing so, Jesus became the Second Adam, reversing the curse of death, as validated by his resurrection (1 Cor 15:21–22).

In the same way that the Immaculate Conception confirms Jesus' divinity and establishes credibility with God, Jesus' innocent suffering on the cross confirms his humanity and status as God's chose sacrifice for our sins.

Loving Father, Beloved Son, Holy Spirit. We praise you for sharing yourself with us in the person of Jesus of Nazareth and stepping into history. Your silent suffering on the cross shouts your love into our fallen world. Thank you for modeling a perfect life; bearing our sins on the cross; and granting us resurrection peace. In Jesus' name, Amen.

Questions

1. How do we know from the Apostle's Creed that Jesus actually lived?

2.   What are two proofs that Pilot (and Jesus) actually lived?

3.   Who testified to Jesus' innocence? Why was Jesus not simply released?

4.   What was the charge against Jesus? What was the penalty?

5.   What kind of execution was crucifixion? How did Jewish tradition interpret it?

6.   How did Jesus substitute for the penalty of sin?

7.   Why should we care about Jesus' suffering?

DAY 11: *Hell*

"he descended to hell."✝

What is hell?

Scripture has many colorful terms that translate into the English word for hell. Among them are: Sheol (OT only; 65 verses), the Abyss (or bottomless pit; 13), Gehenna (NT only; 11), Hades (9), Abaddon (7), and place of darkness (1). Jesus' favorite term was Gehenna which refers to a dump in the Valley of Hinnom near Jerusalem where garbage was burned[1].

The list of words for hell here is, however, incomplete because most of the colorful expressions referring to hell are metaphorical. For example, an angel in Revelation 18:2 cries out in John's vision:

> *"Fallen, fallen is Babylon the great! She has become a dwelling place for demons, a haunt for every unclean spirit, a haunt for every unclean bird, a haunt for every unclean and detestable beast . . ."*

In other words, hell is a kind of prison reserved for the demons, the sinful, and the ritually unclean—all sorts of creatures that oppose heaven and God himself (Isa 7:11). Hell is

---

1 γέεννα (BDAG 1606).

sealed for everyone, except for God (Job 26:6).

Non-biblical visions of hell also exist. For example, C.S. Lewis (1973, 10–11) pictures hell as a place where people voluntarily move further and further apart.

So why does Jesus go to hell for three days?

The culturally expected answer in the first century would have been that Jesus was dead and that was where dead people went. We read, for example: *"For in death there is no remembrance of you; in Sheol who will give you praise?" (Ps 6:5)* But Jesus was not just another dead guy!

A better answer is that with the crucifixion, God's sovereignty over heaven and earth—including hell—was confirmed (Ps 139:8). This might explain, for example, why Jesus' death was accompanied by an earthquake and by resurrection of dead saints from tombs in Jerusalem (Matt 27:51–54)[2].

The best answer to the question is that the reason why Jesus descended into hell remains a mystery. But, hell's existence is no longer a mystery—Jesus went there.

Sovereign Lord. God of the living and the dead. Thank you for caring enough for us that you sent Jesus to hell and back for our

---

2 Of course, later with the resurrection death and Hades itself were overthrown.

benefit. Keep our hearts and minds safe from a fascination with evil. Set our minds on heaven so that our hearts may rest with you, now and always. In the name of the Father, the Son, and the Holy Spirit, Amen.

Questions

1.   Why did Jesus descend into hell for three days?

2.   What are some of the names for hell in scripture? Which one did Jesus use and what does it refer to?

3.   What is unique about Matthew's account of Jesus' death?

4.   Does hell exist? How do we know?

DAY 12: Resurrection

"The third day he rose again from the dead."✝

W hy should we believe in the resurrection?

The truth of the resurrection became the most important confession of the early church. In John's Gospel faith consists, primarily, in believing in the resurrection (John 20:25–29). Paul's letter to the Romans states it plainly: *"if you confess with your mouth that Jesus is Lord and believe in your heart that God raised him from the dead, you will be saved"* *(Rom 10:9).* Paul knew this truth first hand because the risen Christ appeared to him on the road to Damascus—a story recorded three times in the Book of Acts[1]. At one point, the risen Christ appears to more than five hundred witnesses in just one setting (1 Cor 15:6).

The resurrection event changed the Apostle's lives forever. Ten of the eleven faithful apostles died a martyr's death[2]. The fact that they were willing to die for their beliefs is strong historical evidence for the truth of the resurrection.

Peter's sermon at Pentecost in Jerusalem speaks of both

---

1 Paul's conversion was so powerful that he ceased being one of the church's chief persecutors and he became one of the early church's strongest evangelists (Acts 8:3). Also see: Acts 8:3–5, 22:6–8, and 26:13–15.

2 The Apostle John was the only one of the eleven faithful disciples that did not die a martyr (Fox and Chadwick 2001, 10).

the prophecy of the resurrection and the eye witness accounts. Peter cites this prophecy: *"For you will not abandon my soul to Sheol, or let your holy one see corruption" (Ps 16:10)*. The original context of the Psalm points to King David[1], but Peter, as an apostle, correctly interprets the *"holy one"* as referring also to Jesus (Acts 2:27–31). Peter's next statement is most telling: *"This Jesus God raised up, and of that we all are witnesses." (Acts 2:32)* Peter's argument was both truthful and compelling because it convinced more than three thousand people to be baptised that day (Acts 2:41).

At least three reasons motivate us to believe in the resurrection. The first reason was given by Paul: *"if Christ has not been raised, your faith is futile and you are still in your sins." (1 Cor 15:17)* We obtain forgiveness from God only because of Christ's perfect sacrifice as the Lamb of God. A second reason follows from the first. Jesus' resurrection makes our resurrection and eternal life possible. A third reason is that in the resurrection God attested Jesus as the Christ (Acts 17:31). Jesus' path in life, death, and resurrection then becomes the template for

---

1 The verse is a Hebrew doublet. The two parts repeat the same thought. Therefore, holy one refers to my soul.

our faith and the only source of our salvation (Phil 3:10–11).

Heavenly Father. We praise you for Christ's faithful example in life, death, and resurrection. In the power of your Holy Spirit, banish our doubt; prosper our faith; heal our sin-sick souls; and grant us peace. In Jesus's name, Amen.

Questions

1. What is the evidence for the resurrection?

2. What evidence did Peter cite in his sermon on the Day of Pentecost?

3. What was the confession of the early church?

4. What evidence do we have from the life of Saul?

5. What are three reasons why the resurrection is important to us?

DAY 13: Ascension

"He ascended to heaven and is seated at the right hand of God the Father almighty."✞

*T*he ascension is where Jesus commissions the church.

The Gospels of Mark and Luke briefly describe Christ's ascension. For example, Mark reports the ascension with these words: *"So then the Lord Jesus, after he had spoken to them, was taken up into heaven and sat down at the right hand of God." (Mark 16:19)* Luke 24:50 places the ascension near Bethany. The Gospel of Matthew ends, not with the ascension, but with the Great Commission[1] while the Gospel of John focuses more on specific instructions to given to the disciples[2].

The key to understanding the ascension arises in the Book of Acts, which outlines a parallel between Jesus' work and the work of the disciples. In life on earth and in life after death, Christ is our model.

Just like Christ asserts God's sovereignty over heaven and hell in his death on the cross, the disciples are commis-

---

1 *"Go therefore and make disciples of all nations, baptizing them in the name of the Father and of the Son and of the Holy Spirit, teaching them to observe all that I have commanded you. And behold, I am with you always, to the end of the age." (Matt 28:19–20)*

2 For example: *"Jesus said to him [Peter],' If it is my will that he remain until I come, what is that to you? You follow me!'" (John 21:22)*

sioned to assert God's sovereignty over the earth after the ascension. Just before he ascended, Jesus said:

> . . . *But you will receive power when the Holy Spirit has come upon you, and you will be my witnesses in Jerusalem and in all Judea and Samaria, and to the end of the earth.* (Acts 1:8)

This parallel ministry is also discussed in John's Gospel: "*As the Father has sent me, even so I am sending you.*" *(John 20:21)* We see parallel language also in the Lord's Prayer: "*Your kingdom come, your will be done, on earth as it is in heaven.*" *(Matt 6:10)*[3]

Christ's ascension also includes one of the lighter moments in scripture:

> *And when he [Jesus] had said these things, as they were looking on, he was lifted up, and a cloud took him out of their sight. And while they were gazing into heaven as he went, behold, two men stood by them in white robes, and said, "Men of Galilee, why do you stand looking into heaven? This Jesus, who was taken up from you into heaven, will come in the same way as you saw him go into heaven." (Acts 1:9–11)*

In other words, Christians are not supposed to leave

---

3 Also: Luke 24:49, Acts 1:4, and John 14:26. The Great Commission in Matt 28:18–20 also links heaven and earth in evangelism.

their heads in the clouds and stare off into space![1] What seems humorous is actually serious and includes a warning. Disciples who leave their heads in the clouds are warned that Christ will return, which is, perhaps, an allusion to the parable of the talents that includes judgment of slothful servants (Matt 25:14–28).

The ascension links us to Christ's work in heaven. The Book of Hebrews describes Jesus' work as a high priest in heaven interceding in prayer for us (Heb 8:1–2). It should come as great comfort that Jesus, who we know, will sit in judgment when we appear before God's judgment seat[2]. If heaven works like the North Star in our Christian walk, then Christ's ongoing work in heaven is the heart of that star (Alcorn 2006, xi). And Christ inspires the church's work here on earth.

Almighty God. We praise you for the assurance of your love for us that we have in Jesus Christ. Following your lead, soften our hearts, sharpen our minds and strengthen our hands for your

---

1 C. S. Lewis (2001, 134) observed: *"If you read history you will find that the Christians who did most for the present world were just those who thought most of the next."*

2 As the Apostle Paul told the Athenians: *"The times of ignorance God overlooked, but now he commands all people everywhere to repent, because he has fixed a day on which he will judge the world in righteousness by a man whom he has appointed; and of this he has given assurance to all by raising him from the dead." (Acts 17:30–31)*

service. In the power of your Holy Spirit, empower us to be faithful stewards of the Gospel story. In Jesus' precious name, Amen.

Questions

1.   Where is the ascension mentioned in scripture and what is context?

2.   How are Christ's work and our work linked?

3.   Give an example of scriptural humor. What does it teach?

4.   Why does Christ's high priestly work in heaven give comfort to us?

DAY 14: *Judgment*

"From there he will come to judge the living and the dead."✝

*A*re you ready for your final exam?

When I taught in the university, my final exam was never a surprise. The week before the final I would pass out ten questions as homework and announce that five of these questions would be on the final exam. Now these were not easy questions—my questions were designed to encourage my students to master the subject. My good students invariably typed up answers to all ten questions and simply turn all of them in on the day of the examination; my lazy students showed up empty handed and unprepared to answer the questions.

God's judgment works a bit like a take-home exam. We know the questions from scripture and from our ongoing relationship with God and His people, the church. Jesus' commands and teaching are not a surprise.

So why does judgment create such drama?

One answer comes from a surprising source. Immanuel Kant observed that an evil person was not one who wills evil, but one who secretly exempts themselves from judgment, perhaps hoping that God does not exist (Arendt 1992, 17)[1].

Another answer is that many people avoid making decisions, hoping that they can escape accountability. Hannah Arendt was a German Jew who, having escaped Nazi death camps before coming to America, was asked to report on the Adolf Eichmann trial in Jerusalem (1961) for the New Yorker magazine. Eichmann was the German officer during the Second World War who organized Adolf Hitler's program of extermination of the Jews known as the "Final Solution". Arendt attended the trial expecting to see a hateful, anti-Semite only to discover that Eichmann was more of a petty bureaucrat, someone unable to think for himself. In the case of Eichmann, the face of evil was that of someone unable or unwilling to think for themselves (Arendt 1992, 97–101).

Why do we care about the Hannah Arendt story? Because we worship a righteous judge in heaven who expects that we will exercise sound judgment here on earth. We must be good stewards of the wisdom and knowledge of truth entrusted us. Not judging is not an option—robotic thinkers walk the path of Adolf Eichmann, not the path of Jesus Christ. We are

---

1 Kant further speculated that true justice requires that our lives be examined in their entirety which is only possible if resurrection and eternal, impartial judge exist. Therefore, justice and accountability require both eternal life and God!

accountable both for judgments we make and those we refuse to make.

So what does God's judgment look like?

The picture of God as a divine judge brings to mind the story of King Solomon and the two prostitutes. Both women had babies but when one baby died the women fought over the living child. Solomon tested the hearts of the women by threatening the child with death. In doing so, the women revealed their true feelings for the child and he was able to return the child to its rightful mother (1 Kgs 3:16–28).

Just like Solomon, God is a passionate judge who pursues truth and refuses to accept lies at face value[1]. Woe to the person who invites such testing! This is perhaps why the Lord's Prayer includes the petition: *"And lead us not into temptation, but deliver us from evil." (Matt 6:13)*

Almighty Father. Judge of the living and the dead. Compassionate Spirit. May we follow your example and passionately pursue truth and justice. Help us to open our hearts and sharpen our minds. In the power of your Holy Spirit, grant us compassion-

---

1 If you do not like Solomon test, think about the testing of Job who innocently lost everything (Job 1). Or, how about testing of Jesus in the desert? (Luke 4:1–13).

ate hearts for those in need. In Jesus' precious name, Amen.

Questions

1. Why is God's judgment like a take-home exam?

2. According to Immanent Kant, what does an evil person look like?

3. Who was Adolf Eichmann? What was surprising about him?

4. Why must we learn to exercise good judgment?

5. What was the story of King Solomon and the two women? Why do we care?

DAY 15: *The Holy Spirit*

"I believe in the Holy Spirit."✞

Τhe Holy Spirit, sometimes called the Holy Ghost, is the third person of the Trinity. The Holy Spirit goes by a number of names and descriptions in scripture including: Spirit of the Lord (Judg 3:10), Spirit of God (Matt 3:16), Spirit of Truth (John 14:17), Spirit of Life (Rom 8:2), Spirit of the Living God (2 Cor 3:3), Spirit of Wisdom (Eph 1:17), Spirit of Jesus Christ (Phil 1:19), Eternal Spirit (Heb 9:14), Spirit of Glory (1 Pet 4:14), Spirit of Prophecy (Rev 19:10), Helper (John 14:16), and God of Endurance and Encouragement (Rom 15:5).

The wide range of titles suggests that the Holy Spirit plays a wide range of roles and suggests a God of power who is anxious to confer many different spiritual gifts. The Apostle Paul writes:

> *no one can say "Jesus is Lord" except in the Holy Spirit.*
> *Now there are varieties of gifts, but the same Spirit; and*
> *there are varieties of service, but the same Lord; and*
> *there are varieties of activities, but it is the same God*
> *who empowers them all in everyone. (1 Cor 12:3–6)*

By gifting and empowering spiritual gifts, the Holy Spirit makes Christian unity possible because these gifts make the

Christian life, community, and mission service possible.

The Holy Spirit sometimes makes avian (or bird like) appearances. In creation, for example, we witness that: *"the Spirit of God was hovering over the face of the waters." (Gen 1:2)* The word for hovering here in the Hebrew later describes an eagle (Deut 32:11). In all four Gospels, the Holy Spirit descends in baptism on Jesus like a dove—a fitting symbol of God's peace[1]. For this reason, in part, the Holy Spirit is often associated with the sacrament of baptism.

In the Gospel of John, Jesus describes the Holy Spirit saying: *"But the Helper, the Holy Spirit, whom the Father will send in my name, he will teach you all things and bring to your remembrance all that I have said to you." (John 14:26)* The Greek word for helper here transliterates as the Paraclete, which also means advocate, intercessor, and mediator[2]. The verbal form of Paraclete also means to comfort, to encourage, to console, and to exhort[3]. John 14:26 equates the Paraclete to the Holy Spirit.

Although we frequently think of the Holy Spirit in highly personal terms, the supreme act of the Holy Spirit began at

---

1 Matt 3:16, Mark 1:10, Luke 3:22, and John 1:32.
2 (BDAG, 5591).
3 (BDAG, 5590).

Pentecost in the founding of the church. We read:

> *And suddenly there came from heaven a sound like a mighty rushing wind, and it filled the entire house where they were sitting. And divided tongues as of fire appeared to them and rested on each one of them. And they were all filled with the Holy Spirit and began to speak in other tongues as the Spirit gave them utterance. (Acts 2:2–4)*

The word for Holy Spirit in both Hebrew and Greek means both spirit and wind. The church's evangelism and service illustrate the Holy Spirit's continuing provision for reaching the world.

Almighty Father, Beloved Son, Holy Spirit. We praise you for creating and re-creating our world. Bless the church with the Holy Spirit's continuing presence and spiritual gifts that we may minister with power and grace to a fallen world. And in all circumstances grant us peace. In Jesus' precious name, Amen.

Questions

1.   What are some names for the Holy Spirit? What can we learn from them?

2. What is an avian form of the Holy Spirit? Where do we see it at work in scripture?

3. What is a special name for the Holy Spirit?

4. What act of the Holy Spirit is best known?

DAY 16: *The Holy Catholic Church*

*D*oes this phrase, the Holy Catholic Church, mean that we are all Catholic?

The Westminster Confession of faith writes that: *"The catholic or universal church, which is invisible, consists of the whole number of the elect, that have been, are, or shall be gathered into one, under Christ the head." (PCUSA 1999, 6.140)* The universal church includes the elect of the church through the ages, and is invisible in that only God himself knows their identity. The visible church, which we can observe, consists of those elected and those not elected by God. Jesus' parable of the sower makes this point by talking about wheat and the weeds (tares): *"Let both grow together until the harvest, and at harvest time I will tell the reapers, Gather the weeds first and bind them in bundles to be burned, but gather the wheat into my barn." (Matt 13:30)*

The elect are holy—set apart—by God for reasons that God alone understands. Catholic means we are united in diversity (catholic with a small "c"); it does not mean that we are all Roman Catholic (Catholic with a big "C").

The doctrine of election is a necessary condition for the

sovereignty of God to have any real meaning. God created us and Christ redeemed us before we were born, which implies that we cannot earn our creation and redemption (Eph 2:1–10). Our total dependence on God for salvation becomes obvious when we truly acknowledge and grieve the sin in our lives. Although our inclination to sin has been passed down from Adam and Eve, we also actively sin for ourselves. It is like our spiritual ancestors chose to live in enemy territory, and we grew up living there speaking the local dialect[1].

So, none of us have earned our creation or our redemption. The gift of faith is both free and priceless. The mystery of election is that we do not know who is saved or why. Jesus simply said: *"My sheep hear my voice, and I know them, and they follow me." (John 10:27)*

Our task is to spread the Good News, to pray for the lost, and to trust that God is good, just, and always honors his promises.

God of all wonders. We praise you for creating and redeeming us. Help us to grieve our sin, to trust in your goodness, and to rely on your promises. Heal our brokenness; grant us faith;

---

1 The effect of this personal sin becomes most obvious when we have children of our own and experience first-hand how our sin and brokenness impacts them.

restore us as children of God. In the power of your Holy Spirit, grant us spiritual gifts for ministry and a willingness to use them. In Jesus' name, Amen.

Questions

1.   What does catholic mean? How does it relate to the visible and invisible church?

2.   Who are the elect? How does the doctrine of election relate to God's sovereignty?

3.   What are two things outside our control?

4.   Why are we totally dependent on God? What is the role of trust?

DAY 17: *The Communion of Saints*

The phrase, communion of the saints, connotes two things: unity and holiness. A communion is a fellowship and, in the Christian context, implies a table fellowship—the Lord's Supper. In Greek, saint and *holy one* are the same word. Unity in holiness is rare these days.

The Garden of Eden was initially a picture of peace and unity. Adam, Eve, and God were all at peace with one another (Gen 2). Satan broke this unity with temptation that led to sin (Gen 3). After leaving Eden, the death of Abel at the hands of his brother, Cain, amplified the family disunity. Disunity was further magnified in the line of Cain which led to Lamech, who introduced polygamy, further murder, and revenge killing. In a nutshell, sin broke our relationship with God, with one another, with our communities, and with nature itself.

To combat this disunity, Adam and Eve had a third son, Seth, who replaced Abel as the righteous son of Adam (Gen 4). Seth was "fathered" in his image of his father, Adam, much like Adam was created in God's image (Gen 5:1–3). The righteous line of Seth maintained a special relationship with God and became a living witness to the world. Being this living witness was the mission of Abraham (Gen 12:2), the nation of Israel (Isa

2:1–5), and, after Pentecost, the mission of the New Covenant community of Jesus that became the church (Acts 1:8).

Jesus taught unity. He said: *"By this all people will know that you are my disciples, if you have love for one another." (John 13:35)* He encouraged the disciples to minister in pairs (Luke 10:1). Shared ministry was not only a lesson in evangelism; it was a lesson in unity. It is no surprise then to hear how Jesus remarked at the report of the seventy-two disciples: *"I saw Satan fall like lightning from heaven." (Luke 10:18)*

C.S. Lewis (1973, 10–11) gives a visual image of disunity when he pictures hell as a place where people move further and further apart. At its best, the church is a place where people move closer and closer together. In the tradition of Seth, the church stands being created in the image of God through the Holy Spirit at Pentecost. The church's sense of community, post Pentecost, is the metaphorical return to Eden (Acts 2:42–45).

The Apostle Paul painted an image of unity when he likened the church to the body with many parts. He observed: *"if the ear should say, 'Because I am not an eye, I do not belong to the body,' that would not make it any less a part of the body."* *(1 Cor 12:16)* We are all special and yet differ in the spirit gifts that we bring to the church through the Holy Spirit. This is why we celebrate the gifts of others. For our unity is in Christ and Christ's mission, not in our idiosyncrasies and differences. Still, the need for reconciliation is evidence that our differences are real and ongoing.

Loving Father. Beloved Son. Compassionate Spirit. We praise you for your example of unity in holiness. Set us apart in holiness; draw us together. Encourage us to use our spiritual gifts for the common good and to rejoice when others do too. In Jesus' precious name, Amen.

Questions

1.   What is the original picture of unity? How did disunity arise?

2.   Who was Seth? Why was there a need for a righteous family line in Genesis?

3.   What did Jesus teach about unity?

4.   How did C.S. Lewis visualize hell? How does his image of hell relate to the church?

5.   What was the Apostle Paul's image of unity?

DAY 18: Forgiveness of Sins

Why is forgiveness a sign of God's presence? Scripture attests to God's overwhelming love for us and willingness to forgive our sins. Even after God discovers the sin of Adam and Eve, he does not immediately impose a death sentence on them, as previously warned; instead, he outfits them with clothes like a mother preparing her first grader for school[1]. Similarly after Cain murders Abel, God offers Cain grace, protecting him from revenge (Gen 4:15).

The link between God's love and forgiveness allows the psalmist to write:

> Bless the LORD, O my soul, and forget not all his benefits, who forgives all your iniquity, who heals all your diseases, who redeems your life from the pit, who crowns you with steadfast love and mercy. (Ps 103:2–4)

So if God's forgiveness was already well-attested in the Old Testament, why did Jesus need to die on the cross?

Part of the answer is to observe that God's forgiveness of Adam, Eve, and Cain was providentially incomplete. All three were still cursed; all three still left the presence of God. Christ's

1 Gen 2:17; 3:21. God imposed a consequence for sin on Adam and Eve, but also left them with a "positive conclusion" so that they might learn from their mistake and not be embittered (Turansky and Miller (2013, 130–131).

work on the cross was comprehensive, a re-creation event, as the Apostle Paul writes:

> Therefore, if anyone is in Christ, he is a new creation. The old has passed away; behold, the new has come. All this is from God, who through Christ reconciled us to himself and gave us the ministry of reconciliation; that is, in Christ God was reconciling the world to himself, not counting their trespasses against them, and entrusting to us the message of reconciliation. (2 Cor 5:17–19)

Christ reconciled us with God so we should reconcile with one another. With Adam, Eve, and Cain, none of this happens.

Some psychologists look at forgiveness as a reframing event. Reframing occurs when new meaning is attached to a negative experience. For example, psychoanalyst Victor Frankl, when confined to a concentration camp during the Second World War, focused his mind on preparing the lectures that he would give after the war on his camp experience. In reframing his persecution, Frankl was able to survive the camp when others gave up hope and died (Rosen 1982, 141). Reframing falls short of forgiveness because it focuses solely on the individual, neglecting the relationship among individuals and with God.

When God forgives our sin, in a sense we reframe

our self-image from rebel to child of God. The greater the sin forgiven, the deeper the transformation enabled. Forgiveness releases us from death row condemnation and allows us to be reconciled with God, those we sin against, and all of creation. When we then forgive others, we become ambassadors for Christ in this magnificent reconciliation project (2 Cor 5:20).

Loving Father. Beloved Son. Forgiving Spirit. We praise you for your love and forgiveness. Redeem us from our sin; empower our lives with new meaning. In the power of your Holy Spirit, grant us new status as children of God and allow us to enter your work of reconciliation. In Jesus' precious name, Amen.

Questions

1.   What acts of grace and forgiveness do we read about in Genesis? How was God's forgiveness of Adam, Eve, and Cain incomplete?

2.   Why are love and forgiveness so closely tied together?

3.   How was Christ's reconciliation more complete forgiveness?

4.   How does reframing differ from forgiveness?

5.   What does forgiveness have to do with death row?

DAY 19: *Resurrection of the Body*

One big anxiety that amputees experience is that lost body parts embody their identity in ways that must now change. The pain is particularly acute when the body part is associated with a beloved activity. Our hearts go out, for example, to the runner who loses a leg or the brilliant researcher who develops Alzheimer's disease. Our body is part of our identity.

God knows who we are and feels our pain—to be human is to be whole in body, mind, and spirit.

Jesus raised the widow's son out of compassion (Luke 7:13) and he wept before raising Lazarus from the dead (John 11:35). How compassionate would Jesus have been if he had raised the widow's son from the dead only to have the son live on as a paraplegic? Or if Jesus raised Lazarus from the dead but left him mentally handicapped?

During my time as a chaplain intern, I knew a dear woman who had been resuscitated after her heart stopped for eight minutes. The resuscitation left her afflicted with dementia and forced to live in a lock-down, Alzheimer's unit. The affliction left her family guilt ridden and torn over their decision to resuscitate her.

Resuscitation leaves scars. Scripture reports that the

widow's son and Lazarus were returned to health without scars. Consequently, Jesus did not resuscitate them; he re-created them as only God can[1].

Resurrection is an act of grace—bodily resurrection completes the compassion.

Jesus was bodily resurrected. When the resurrected Christ appeared before the disciples in Jerusalem, he asked for something to eat; the disciples gave him a piece of broiled fish and he ate it (Luke 24:41–43). Furthermore, Christ's compassion for his own disciples, who had deserted him, reveals that Jesus, in his perfection, did not harbor the deep emotional scars that might normally accompany the trauma that he experienced (John 21:17).

Consider the alternative. What if Jesus had been raised only spiritually, how long would he continue to empathize with us? Or what if Jesus harbored grievous handicaps or emotional scares? Would he still have pity on the rest of us? Would we really want to stand before such a scarred and potentially vengeful judge?

Christ's resurrection was a re-creation, not resuscitation, event. Christ's resurrection gives us hope because our judge is

1 Meredith Kline (2006, 220–21) uses the term re-creation in reference to the flood narrative and sees this idea already present in 2 Pet 3:5–7. In other words, Noah was a second Adam even before Christ.

healthy and whole. He is still human and he harbors no grievances.

God of all compassion. We praise you for sharing yourself in the person of Jesus of Nazareth who in life served as a role model for sinners, in death ransomed us from the power of sin, and in resurrection left us with the hope of glory. Bind our wounds; heal our scars; raise us from death. Grant us awareness of your presence so that we also can be fully present to those around us. In the power of your Holy Spirit, make us whole people. In Jesus' precious name, Amen.

Questions

1. How does our body factor into our identity? How do we know that God is compassionate?

2. How does resurrection differ from resuscitation? What does it mean to be re-created? Why is resurrection an act of grace?

3. How do we know that Jesus was truly resurrected?

4. Why does bodily resurrection give us hope?

DAY 20: *Everlasting Life*

*W*hat is eternal life?

Our life in Christ is a journey which begins sinful and finite, but progresses towards holy and eternal[1]. The progress towards eternal life requires both spiritual restoration and bodily healing.

We normally think of God's eternal nature before his holiness. This first aspect of eternal life is quantitative—overcoming death to live eternally with God. However, this line of thinking is backwards: death is the penalty for sin. In other words, sin causes death. God's forgiveness in Christ removes the sin, removes the penalty of death, and makes eternal life possible[2].

Unfortunately, sin not only triggers a death penalty; it pollutes us and damages our relationships. For example, the Apostle Paul's conversion included God's forgiveness, but Paul's ravaging of the church was not easily forgotten (Acts 9:10–15). Likewise, the murderer who is forgiven has his guilt removed, but the life taken has not been restored and his broken relation-

---

1 Because of original sin, we are cut off from God at birth by sin and destined to die because of sin's penalty—death. In Christ, we see the image of a holy and eternal God. Christ both affects our moral improvement (sinful to holy) and bodily healing (mortal to immortal).

2 John 3:36; Rom 10:9–10.

ships remain broken.

Consequently, the second aspect of eternal life is qualitative—removing sin's pollution and reconciling our relationships through Christ. The Apostle John writes: *"this is eternal life that they may know you the one, true God and the one who you sent, Jesus Christ." (John 17:3; my translation).* We are a new creation in Christ and reconciled to Him, but reconciliation has two parts. The first part is reconciliation with God and it is completed with the work of Christ. The second part is reconciliation with brothers and sisters against whom we sinned (2 Cor 5:17–20). This final stage in reconciliation, which can only be completed with and through the power of the Holy Spirit, requires both sanctification of the individual and participation of the church. This is also area where the spiritual disciplines can focus most productively.

Eternal life, accordingly, begins with the work of Christ (justification and reconciliation with God), but continues in the work of the church (reconciliation with those we have sinned against). The Good News is that in Christ and through the Holy Spirit God's work in us will be complete.

Holy and Compassionate Father. We praise you for creating

us in your image. We praise you for the gift of eternal life and for the gift of your son, Jesus Christ. In the power of your Holy Spirit, grant us strength for each day. Forgive our sin; heal our hearts; reconcile us with you and with each other. In Jesus' precious name, Amen.

Questions

1. What is our life's journey? How does creation fit in?

2. What are two aspects of the divine image?

3. What does God's forgiveness in Christ accomplish?

4. What effects of sin remain even after forgiveness?

5. What are two parts to the qualitative aspect of eternal life?

THE LORD'S PRAYER

Our Father in Heaven, Hallowed be your Name. Your Kingdom Come, Your Will be Done, on Earth as it is in Heaven. Give us this Day our Daily Bread, And Forgive us our Debts, as We also have Forgiven our Debtors. And Lead us not into Temptation, but Deliver us from Evil." (Matt 6:9–13)

The Lord's Prayer helps define our identity in Christ and to focus on the question: WHO ARE WE? The answer given is that we are debtors—vassals (subordinate kings)[1]—who are in need of daily bread and are easily tempted.

The Lord's Prayer also helps us answer the other three big philosophical questions:

- WHO IS GOD? He is our father who is the King of kings—the Suzerain—living in heaven.

- WHAT DO WE DO ABOUT IT? We praise God's name.

- HOW DO WE KNOW? The Bible records the Lord's Prayer twice[2].

Teaching prayer is difficult. Our prayers reflect our understanding of theology and how we practice it—our personal spirituality[3]. If we neglect theology, then our walk with the Lord may be uninformed and our prayers may reduce to mimicing someone else's prayer or to babble[4].

The Lord's Prayer reveals Jesus' own theology and pro-

---

1 Day 35 contains a more detailed discussion of vassals and suzerains.

2 See: Matt 6:9–13 and Luke 11:2–4. In this discussion, I follow the Matt version of the Lord's Prayer because it is a bit more complete. The scriptural text differs slightly from that used in worship because of the traditions of the church.

3 Simon Chan (1998, 16).

4 This is probably what Jesus means when he says: *"And when you pray, do not heap up empty phrases as the Gentiles do, for they think that they will be heard for their many words."* (Matt 6:7)

vides us an important template for prayer. The hope is that, by employing Jesus' template, we may develop a personal theology through study, personal prayer, and being attentive to the Holy Spirit's work in our lives.

DAY 21: *What is your attitude in prayer?*

"And he said, Abba, Father, all things are possible for you. Remove this cup from me. Yet not what I will, but what you will." (Mark 14:36)

*T*he Lord's Prayer radically changed the disciples' attitudes about prayer.

To understand how much attitudes had to change, think about how a first century Jew would view Jesus' prayer. In the Lord's Prayer, we, metaphorically, enter the city of Jerusalem; go through ritual purification to the outer courts of the temple, step into the Holy place, and pull back the veil of the Holy of Holies. Then, at the mercy seat of the Ark of the Covenant, we put on the ephod[1] of the high priest and begin to pray, not to YHWH, but to Daddy! Talk about radical!

If this metaphor for prayer seems far-fetched, consider Paul's last trip to Jerusalem. Paul arrived in the city in the company of fellow believers (gentiles), probably Greeks from Corinth (1 Cor 16:3). When he entered the temple a riot broke out as Jews who had seen him in the city accused Paul of bringing a gentile into the temple. Paul escaped with his life from this riot only because the Roman guards rescued him (Acts 21:26–

[1]A ceremonial garment worn by the high priest described in Exod 28.

32). This story underscores the point that it was unthinkable, to a Jew, that anyone could enter God's presence—especially in the Temple—without proper cleansing, preparation, and authority.

What is your attitude in prayer? Are you reverent or cavalier in approaching God? Although the temple veil was torn when Christ died on the cross[2], God is still holy and we can approach the mercy seat only by the invitation of Christ. Respecting God's boundaries is an important step in approaching prayer. *"Be holy because I am holy" (Lev 11:44)* says the Lord God.

Almighty God, beloved Son, Holy Spirit. Thank you for allowing us to enter into your presence to pray and for being present in our daily lives. Illuminate our minds; consecrate our hearts. Help us to be fully present with each other and with you in prayer. In Jesus' name, Amen.

Questions

1. Why was the Lord's Prayer shocking to a first century Jew?

2. What were God's boundaries in the layout of the temple?

3. What is a proper attitude in prayer? Why?

2 The splitting of the temple veil is recorded in all three of the synoptic Gospels (Matt 27:51; Mark 15:38; and Luke 23:45). Roman armies destroyed the temple during a Jewish uprising in AD 70.

4.   Why is it hard to learn to pray?

5.   Why is the Lord's Prayer a surprisingly theological template?

DAY 22: *Our Heavenly Father*

And when you pray, do not heap up empty phrases as the Gentiles do, for they think that they will be heard for their many words. Do not be like them, for your Father knows what you need before you ask him. Pray then like this: Our Father in heaven . . . (Matt 6:7–9)

*T*he first phrase in the Lord's Prayer is: *"Our Father".* We come before God as a community under a sovereign God. Addressing God as father focuses primarily on God's sovereignty, not God's gender[1]. God is a benevolent sovereign who desires relational intimacy with his children. He is not a buddy god or a needy god that can be manipulated. Rather, we depend on God for everyday bread—not the other way around.

For human fathers who are not good role models, scripture reminds us that God is a father to the fatherless (Ps 68:5). Scripture is not just "turning a phrase" here. One consequence of slavery in Egypt and later in Babylon was illegitimacy, which kept many Jewish children from ever meeting their fathers. The word, orphan, is used in over fifty verses in scripture—eleven times in the book of Deuteronomy alone. Jesus himself assures

---

1 The image of God as our father makes a statement about His character. God is spirit; being neither male or female.

us: *"I will not leave you as orphans; I will come to you." (John 14:18)* Our Heavenly Father's love for us, His children, inspires our human fathers, not the other way around.

Christian spirituality has a communal character—it is not my spirituality; it is our spirituality. In baptism, for example, we are presented to God and to the church. In communion, we remember our baptism and celebrate our covenantal relationship with God and with one another. We can enjoy solitude with God while recognizing the vital role our community of faith has in shaping our relationship with God. In turn, we know God better as we love one another.

The communal aspect of God's intimacy implies that our spirituality is not focused just on warm, fuzzy feelings. Ours is not a consumer spirituality. Great panoramas, great music, great poetry, great architecture, and great intellectual achievements all point to God, but our spirituality is inherently relational. We are most likely to see God's face in the faces of those around us.

Jesus' stories and parables drive this point home:

> *So if you are offering your gift at the altar and there remember that your brother has something against you, leave your gift there before the altar and go. First*

be reconciled to your brother, and then come and offer

your gift. (Matt 5:23–24)

Our spiritual identity is in a sovereign God and in right relationships with His people. The two are inexplicably bound together.

The doctrine of the Trinity reinforces this point. Every conversation is three-way. It is always you, me, and God. God is above us, between us, and within us. In God's transcendence, God is all powerful and in control. In the incarnation of Jesus Christ, God shares our pain and provides us a role model. In the Holy Spirit's presence, God comforts and guides us. We are in relationship with God in three persons. Our identity is defined uniquely and independently in relation to each of these three persons of the Trinity (Miner 2007, 112).

But why is the Lord's Prayer addressed to heaven? The obvious answer is that heaven is God's home address. Another obvious answer is that heaven clarifies which father we are talking about!

Notice that almost all the petitions in the Lord's Prayer center on God, not us. Do we listen for God's voice? Are we approaching our sovereign God in appropriate humility?

Heavenly Father. Thank you for making yourself available to us in the person of Jesus Christ and through the person and ministry of the Holy Spirit. Root out the pride in us; give us listening ears; sanctify our prayer, our lives, and our worship. Guide us in our parenting and family relations. In Jesus' name, Amen.

Questions

1.   What does it mean that God is sovereign in our lives?

2.   Why does scripture describe God as the father to the fatherless?

3.   In what way is Christian spirituality sacramental in character?

4.   How does God's sovereign power reduce the chaos in our lives?

DAY 23: *Praise the Name*

"Pray then like this: Our Father in heaven, hallowed be your name." (Matt 6:9)

*T*he Lord's Prayer reminds us to honor God's name in keeping with the Third Commandment—do not take the Lord's name in vain—because all the other commandments are leveraged on it.

Why keep the other commandments, if we dishonor God's name?

The practical implications of honoring God arise because we are created in God's image. Because we are created in the image of God, human life has intrinsic value—value in itself that does not change with life events. Because life has intrinsic value, we cannot accept discrimination, injustice, abuse, mistreatment of prisoners, weapons of mass destruction, euthanasia, abortion, designer babies, and a host of other detestable practices. Our human rights—a measure reflecting intrinsic value—exist because we are created in the image of a Holy God.

Our capitalist society focuses, not on intrinsic values, but on market values. Market values change with circumstances—they are volatile. Your value as a person implicitly depends on your productivity. If you are young, old, or unable to work, then you are a dependent—a burden on working people. The focus on market values inherently disrespects God's image. When God is not honored; neither are we.

The strong influence of market values on our self-image explains, in part, is why depression rates tend to be highest among population groups—like the young adults and the senior citizens—who are unable to work. The rate of depression, suicide, anxiety disorders, addictions, and divorce appear to be correlated, in part, with changing job prospects.

When God's name is dishonored, we also become more prone to idolatry (Rom 1:21–23). Why worship the God of the Bible, when my income and status in society depends more on my family legacy, education, and hard work? So I naturally run to all sorts of substitutes for God that work, like insurance, to manage the ups and downs of life. Alternatively, I can obsess about the security of my home, my spouse, and my children.

The implications of honoring the name of God come together in the debate over euthanasia—the right to die. If my self-image and my dignity in society are both increasingly subjected to the same market values, then I will surrender myself to assisted suicide precisely when I need support from my family.

And, of course, they will agree because I have become a burden both financially and emotionally. Consequently, euthanasia is evil mascarading as compassion. We are created in the image of a holy God who declares that life is good and sacred (Gen 1:31).

Give glory to God. Honor the NAME above all names. You are created in God's image.

Sovereign Father, lover of our souls, compassionate spirit. Holy, holy, holy is Your name. We praise you for creating us in Your image and loving us intrinisically, just as we are. Grant us the eyes to see others as You see them. Give us ears that hear Your voice above the crowds screaming for our attention. In the precious name of Jesus, Amen.

Questions

1.   How are human dignity and human rights tied to honoring God's name?

2.   What is the implication of being created in the image of God?

3.   What is the difference between intrinsic and market value? Why do we care?

4.   What are some outcomes of dishonoring God?

5.   How do you define idolatry? How does idolatry relate to honoring God's name?

DAY 24: *On Earth as in Heaven*

"Your kingdom come, your will be done, on earth as it is in heaven." (Matt 6:10)

*T*he next two phrases in Jesus' prayer—*"Your kingdom come, your will be done, on earth as it is in heaven"*—are one sentence in the Greek text. These phases repeat the same thought in different ways. Together they express, in a highly emphatic way, the idea that we want God's desires to prevail in our lives, not ours. With this prayer, the disciple radically commits heart and mind to the attainment of God's holy kingdom on earth.

The synoptic Gospels begin citing John the Baptist's famous phrase: *"Repent, for the kingdom of heaven is at hand."* *(Matt 3:2)* In the gospel of Matthew, John the Baptist introduces the phrase, kingdom of heaven, while Jesus introduces the phrase, kingdom of God, in the gospels of Mark and Luke. Thus, while the Baptist focused on judgment, Jesus' stressed salvation (Matt 3:10; 4:23).

Where does this kingdom language come from?[1]

This kingdom language hints at a restoration of the

1 Strassen and Gushee (2003, 22–23, 35) draw a parallel between the beatitudes in Matt 5:3–10 and Isa 61:1–11. Their focus on Isaiah is attractive because Jesus himself cites Isa 61:1 already in his "call sermon" in Nazareth

Garden of Eden. In Eden we see a picture of a world uncorrupted by sin. Adam and Eve rest with God and have access to the Tree of Life. Before the fall, there is no death, no strife, and no corruption. After the fall, there is death, strife, and sin. The kingdom of heaven restores the uncorrupted world of Eden.

One clue of this creation theme echoing Eden is the appearance of strange animal behaviors and spiritual beings. In Isaiah, for example, we read:

> The *wolf shall dwell with the lamb, and the leopard shall lie down with the young goat, and the calf and the lion and the fattened calf together; and a little child shall lead them. (Isa 11:6)*

In Jesus' birth and resurrection accounts, angels appear (e.g. Luke 2:10, 24:4). Not surprisingly, the tree of life returns in the Apostle John's vision of heaven (Rev 22:2).

What are we to conclude? The restoration of Eden in God's new kingdom presents an image of hope. The resurrection of Christ has inaugurated a new kingdom that has not yet been fully realized. In praying for this new kingdom to arrive, we look beyond the present death, strife, and sin to hope for the

---

(Luke 4:18–19).

joy that is to come.

Heavenly Father. We praise you for hope in the future and for the gift of patience. We praise you for the vision of Eden and for the promise of new creation where the fullness of salvation will be revealed and all things made new. For in Christ we know the end of the story. You are our rock and our salvation. To you and you alone be the glory. In the name of the Father, the Son, and the Holy Spirit, Amen.

Questions

1.   Where in scripture does Jesus' kingdom language come from and how do we interpret it?

2.   What clues about a creation theme do we have in Isaiah and Revelation?

3.   What was different before and after the fall into temptation of Adam and Eve?

4.   What does kingdom language suggest about the future?

DAY 25: *God's Will Be Done*

"Your kingdom come, your will be done, on earth as it is in heaven." (Matt 6:10)

Who is in charge of your life?

If God is in charge of your life, then you want to participate in the advancement of God's kingdom and to do his will. Jesus treats them as the same thing. Remember, Hebrew poetry does not rhyme; it doubles. The second phrase repeats the first, but in different words. The more subtle the doubling; the more beautiful the poetry.

To see this doubling, ask yourself a question: how do you know that you have entered a kingdom? A kingdom exists where the king's edicts are obeyed. Jesus prays: *"Your kingdom come, your will be done." (Matt 6:10)*

The third phase in the prayer reinforces the first two. Where does Jesus pray that God's kingdom will be? Let it be a kingdom on earth as in heaven. Where does Jesus pray that God's will be done? Let it be done on earth as in heaven. We aspire that earth be like heaven.

James, the brother of Jesus, echoes this distinction in his contrast between faith and action. He writes simply: *"faith apart from works is dead"* *(Jas 2:26).* Our faith may model heaven, but on earth our actions must reflect it.

Did you notice the subtle reminder of God's creative power in Jesus' prayer? Hint: *"In the beginning, God created the heavens and the earth." (Gen 1:1)* Earth is modeled after heaven in the creation order. It still would be but for the corruption of sin. In praying the Lord's Prayer, we are petitioning God to restore creation and are, in effect, participating in its re-creation.

A Hebrew doublet sometimes takes the form of a negative contrast. In Psalm 1, for example, we read: *"for the LORD knows the way of the righteous [will prosper], but the way of the wicked will perish [not prosper]." (Ps 1:6)* One is a blessing of the law followed; the other is a curse of the law broken. The logic of the pattern invites us to fill in any missing pieces.

In Jesus' prayer, two negative contrasts are implicit. It is your kingdom come; not my kingdom come. It is your will be done; not my will be done. Submission implies choosing God over self.

Heavenly Father, beloved Son, Holy Spirit. We praise you for the hope of the resurrection, the inspiration of heaven, and the gift of your love in both. For we have seen our names carved in

the palms of your hands (John 20:27) and are ashamed. Forgive our sin. Bless us with your presence both day and night. In
Jesus' name, Amen.

Questions

1.   Who is in charge of your life?

2.   What is a Hebrew doublet? In what ways can repetitions

occur?

3.   How do you know that you have entered a new kingdom?

DAY 26: Give Us Daily Bread

"Give us this day our daily bread." (Matt 6:11)

Why ask God for bread and not cake?

When Satan tempted Jesus in the desert to turn a stone into bread, Jesus responded: *"It is written: Man shall not live by bread alone, but by every word that comes from the mouth of God." (Matt 4:4)* Jesus was quoting Deuteronomy 8:3 from a story about God's daily provision of manna, during the nation of Israel's forty year sojourn in the wilderness, which reads:

> *And he humbled you and let you hunger and fed you with manna, which you did not know, nor did your fathers know, that he might make you know that man does not live by bread alone, but man lives by every word that comes from the mouth of the Lord. (Deut 8:3)*

It is humbling to receive only what you need. How many of us only pray for the bare essentials of life?

The Apostle Paul did. He wrote:

> *Not that I am speaking of being in need, for I have learned in whatever situation I am to be content.*

I know how to be brought low, and I know how to abound. In any and every circumstance, I have learned the secret of facing plenty and hunger, abundance and need. I can do all things through him who strengthens me. (Phil 4:11–13)

In asking only for daily bread, Jesus' humble prayer is highly ironic. Why? God's presence is almost always associated with super-abundance—a cake moment. In the Gospel of John, for example, Jesus' first miracle is to turn water into wine—more than a hundred gallons of wine of better quality than expected (John 2:6,10). Later, Jesus feeds five thousand with just a couple of loaves of bread (John 6:5–14). God is not stingy. His trademark is overwhelming generosity.

If you pray for daily bread and get an overwhelming response, then God's presence is revealed. If you pray for cake and get the same result, God's presence is hidden in His generosity.

When the people of Israel were hungry and alone in the wilderness, God provided for them daily with manna. God presence and provision was so meaningful to them that Moses had Aaron place a jar of manna in the Ark of the Covenant (Exod 16:32). By contrast, later when they stood in front of the Promised Land (a cake moment), God's presence was hidden from them and they returned to the wilderness for another forty years (Num 13).

Jesus' bread request suggests even further irony. Jesus was born in Bethlehem. In Hebrew Beth-lehem means: house of bread. Because the Hebrew word, lehem, can also mean food, Jesus may have simply meant for us to ask God to provide food for the day.

Gracious God. Give us the humility to pray for our daily needs. Walk with us during every step we take. Help us to be satisfied in all circumstances and to recognize your presence also in abundance. May we follow your example and be generous with those around us. In the name of the Father, Son, and Holy Spirit, Amen.

Questions

1.	How did Satan tempt Jesus in the desert? What other food temptations come to mind? (Hint: Gen 3; also: Gen 25:29-34)

2.	Why was Jesus' guidance to pray for daily bread ironic?

3.	How did Paul remain content?

4.	How might we recognize God's presence? What is God's trademark?

5.   Do you pray for bread or cake? What was an example of a cake moment in your life?

DAY 27: *You Forgive; We Forgive*

"and forgive us our debts, as we also have forgiven our debtors."
(Matt 6:12)

Why forgive? Why be forgiving?

The simple answer is because Jesus says so. Jesus makes a strong statement on forgiveness immediately following the Lord's Prayer:

> *For if you forgive others their trespasses, your heavenly Father will also forgive you, but if you do not forgive others their trespasses, neither will your Father forgive your trespasses. (Matt 6:14–15)*

The reasoning here is clear—we are to be forgiving people because God has forgiven us. The word for forgiveness in Greek means *let go*.

The Apostle Peter clarified our obligation to forgive when he asked: how many times should we forgive someone who sins against us—seven times? No, said Jesus, seventy seven times—arbitrarily large number that fit the context of Peter's question (Matt 18:21–22)[1]. Jesus then goes on to tell the parable

---

1 Alternative translations, e.g. the New American Standard version, read *seventy times seven.*

of the unforgiving servant (Matt 18:23–35).

The point is that forgiveness aids patience, healing, and redemption.

Forgiveness aids patience. Working with young children or with Alzheimer's patients involves answering repeated questions or dealing with other annoying behaviors. We often find ourselves working with our children and our parents while we juggle other things—including our own exhaustion. If we can forgive people with special needs, then why is it so hard to forgive normal people who are just annoying?[1] A life with no regrets starts with forgiveness.

Forgiveness heals. For example, forgiveness breaks up what psychiatrists call rumination. Extreme forms of rumination occur when a psyche patient obsesses daily for years about stressful or imagined events from the past[2]. Puffed up like that, rumination distracts the patient from normal emotional development and, subsequently, damages relationships. Because we all ruminate, forgiveness heals by helping us focus on life's daily

---

1 Jerry Bridges (1996, 46) writes: *"Do we see them as persons for whom Christ died or as persons who make our lives difficult?"* Christ forgave even his tormentors from the cross (Luke 23:34). If he can love and forgive those who murdered him, surely we can forgive annoying people!.

2 One therapy for rumination is to redirect the patient's focus from the negative memory to a breathe prayer, such as the Jesus prayer. The version of the Jesus prayer that I remember was: Jesus, Son of God, Have mercy on me.

challenges rather than on phantoms from the past[3].

Forgiveness is redemptive. The story of Stephen, the first Christian martyr, is a case in point. Just before he died, Stephen prayed: *"Lord, do not hold this sin against them." (Acts 7:60)* Saul of Taurus witnessed and approved of Stephen's stoning. Better known as Paul, Saul later met the risen Christ on the road to Damascus, was baptized, and became the church's great evangelist. But Paul never forgot Stephen astonishing act of love and linked Stephen to his own call story (Acts 22:20). Were the life and ministry of Paul an answer to Stephen's prayer?

Forgiveness is so radical, so rare, so redemptive that it reveals God's presence among us.

God of all compassion. You are the alpha and the omega, the beginning and the end. We praise you for your example of humility. We thank you for your sacrifice. Help us to confess our sins and forgive those who sin against us. In the power of your Holy Spirit, open our hearts, illumine our minds, and strength-

---

3 Francis MacNutt (2009, 130) cites four types of healing that we can pray for including: repentance, emotional pain, physical healing, and deliverance—healing from spiritual oppression. When we forgive those who have hurt us, we not only offer them healing, we also release our own pain. Unforgiven sin plagues both parties to the sin.

en our hands in your service. In Jesus' name, Amen.

Questions

1.   What lesson does Jesus teach after he finishes teaching the Lord's Prayer? Why is it important?

2.   What does the Apostle Peter ask Jesus?

3.   What can we learn from children, Alzheimer's patients, and annoying people about forgiveness?

4.   How can forgiveness heal and be redemptive?

DAY 28: *Temptation and Evil*

"And lead us not into temptation, but deliver us from evil." (Matt 6:13)

*D*o you ever worry about Satan?

Satan's role in tempting us and promoting evil in the world is found throughout scripture.

In the Garden of Eden, Satan is pictured as a snake who rebels against God and tempts others to sin by rebelling with him[1]. God later advises Cain to be good because, otherwise, sin will strike like a snake crouching at your door (Gen 4:7).

Another important image of Satan is given in Job 1 where Satan is depicted as a ruthless prosecuting attorney in God's court. Satan's cruel lies slander a righteous Job. Still, Satan cannot afflict Job without first seeking God's permission (Job 1:6–12). In spite of Satan's cruelty, Job remains faithful. In the end, God not only acquits him of all of Satan's charges, Job is compensated for his losses (Job 42:10).

In the synoptic gospels, the Holy Spirit leads Jesus into the desert where the devil tempts him[2]. Much like Adam and

---

1 For example, Kline (2006, 302) writes about the people of God and the people of the serpent.

2 Mark 1:12–13 gives a brief over view while Matt 4:1–11 and Luke 4:1–13. The Luke version has the most detail. The second and third questions posed by Satan appear in different order in Matthew and Luke.

Eve are tempted with food, the devil starts by goading a hungry Jesus into turning a stone into bread. The devil tempts Jesus three times. Jesus cites scripture in response to each temptation. In the final temptation, the Devil's temptation starts by mis-quoting scripture, but Jesus corrects the deception and resists the temptation[1].

Like Job and unlike Adam, Jesus remains faithful to God's will in life and in death. Jesus' death on the cross then fulfills the prophecy of Satan's defeat (Gen 3:15) and pays the penalty for sin—we are redeemed. Because the curse of sin is broken, the death penalty for sin has been rescinded (1 Cor 15:22). The resurrection accordingly proves that we have been reconciled with God.

In the Lord's Prayer, Jesus asks us to pray that we not be tempted and that we be delivered from evil. Because Satan must ask permission to tempt us, God can deny that petition and our deliverance is within his power. King David writes: *"Preserve me, O God, for in you I take refuge." (Ps 16:1)* Jesus has promised us that when we turn to him in weakness our salvation is secure

---

1 Each temptation Jesus faces is a challenge facing all Christians, particularly leaders. Henri Nouwen (2002, 7–8) summarizes these leadership challenges as the temptation to be relevant (provide food), to be spectacular (show your divinity), and to be powerful (take charge).

(John 10:29).

Almighty Father. We praise you for creating heaven and earth; creating all that is, was, or will ever be; and creating all things seen and unseen. We look out on your creation and praise your name. Keep us safe in your hands: seal our hearts; strengthen our minds; and shelter our bodies from all evil. In our hour of weakness, may we ever turn only to you. In the name of the Father, the Son, and the Holy Spirit, Amen.

Questions

1. What role does Satan play in the creation and fall narrative in Genesis? How about the Book of Job and the Gospel of Luke?

2. What is the image of sin in Genesis 4?

3. What is the first temptation of Christ in the desert? How does Jesus respond?

4. How are we to respond to temptation and evil? What is the role of prayer?

DAY 29: Doxology

"For thine is the kingdom, and the power, and the glory, for ever. Amen." (Matt 6:13 KJV)

Newer translations of the Bible exclude the doxology: *"For thine is the kingdom, and the power, and the glory, for ever. Amen."*[1] Why?

Jesus gave the disciples the Lord's Prayer to teach them how to pray, not as an obligatory prayer. Three times Jesus repeats the phrase: *"when you pray" (Matt 6:5–7)*. Then, he simply said: *"Pray then like this" (Matt 6:9)*. Jesus offers a pattern for prayer which can be adjusted as needed. The early church loved this prayer and took this advice seriously. The most common addition was to add a doxology and the word, amen, which means *so be it*. Consequently, this addition does not appear in the earliest manuscripts even though churches continue to use it today.

When the reformers began examining the original Greek texts in the fifteenth century, Saint Jerome's Latin translation of the Bible had been used almost exclusively for a thousand years. The Greek New Testament manuscripts immediately available in local libraries were assembled and translated in

[1] For example, the English Standard Version and the New International Version do not include the doxology.

English, German, French, and other European languages. Much later, however, when scholars began to compare the thousands of Greek manuscripts available throughout the world's churches and libraries, they became aware that not all manuscripts were equally ancient. Recent Bible translations focus on the more ancient manuscripts[2].

The older manuscripts exclude the doxology and amen. This is why translations of the Bible made before that discovery include the doxology and amen, while newer translations do not. Hugenberger (1999, 55) observes that the doxology abbreviates a longer doxology found in 1 Chronicles 29:11–13.

Doxology is taken from the Greek word, doxa, which means: *"the condition of being bright or shining, brightness, splendor, radiance"*[3]. Amen is a Hebrew word attributed to Jesus himself that means *truly*. When Jesus says: *"truly, truly I say to you" (John 1:51)*, the Greek text reads—amen, amen—which the Greek transliterates from the Hebrew.

Personal prayer is a Christian distinctive. Jesus taught us how to pray, not exactly what to pray. He wants us to come to <u>him as a commun</u>ity of faith, but he also wants us to approach

2 Metzger and Ehrman (2005) review the New Testament textual history in great detail.

3 *(BDAG 2077, 1)*. For example: *"And an angel of the Lord appeared to them, and the glory (δόξα) of the Lord shone around them, and they were filled with great fear."* (Luke 2:9)

him as individuals. Personal prayer is a Christian distinctive.

Heavenly Father. Beloved Son. Holy Spirit. Thank you for teaching us to pray. Be with us as we take new steps in our journey of faith. Open our minds as you have opened our hearts. In Jesus' name, Amen.

Questions

1.   What is the difference between a prayer pattern and an obligatory prayer?

2.   How has translation of the Bible been affected by the discovery of older Greek manuscripts?

3.   How do we validate our faith?

THE TEN COMMANDMENTS

Blessed is the Man who Walks Not in the Counsel of the Wicked, Nor Stands in the Way of Sinners, Nor Sits in the Seat of Scoffers; But his Delight is in the Law of the LORD, And on His Law he Meditates Day and Night (Ps 1:1–2).

1... You shall have No other gods before Me.

2... You shall Not make for yourself a Carved Image

3... You shall Not take the Name of the LORD your God in Vain

4... Remember the Sabbath day, to Keep it Holy

5... Honor your Father and your Mother

6... You shall Not Murder

7... You shall Not commit Adultery

8... You shall Not Steal

9... You shall Not Bear False Witness against your Neighbor.

10... You shall Not Covet (Exod 20:3–17)

The Ten Commandments help us answer the question: WHAT SHALL WE DO? The answer is straightforward: we should obey God's laws.

The Ten Commandments also help answer the other three fundamental philosophical questions:

- WHO IS GOD? God is the supreme covenant maker who expresses his love for us through concrete guidance.

- WHO ARE WE? We are covenant keepers who accept God's covenant relationship and live accounting to its laws.

- HOW DO WE KNOW? Ten Commandments are recorded and explained in scripture.

Because the law is often discussed in opposition to grace, the role of the Ten Commandments in answering the question of what to do is sometimes confusing. Jesus said that love of neighbor and God summarized the Law and the Prophets (Matt 22:36–40)[1]. Why then do I need law? Aren't I free from law under grace?

The Apostle Paul gives the most direct answer to this question. Our freedom in Christ is the freedom to love our neighbors as ourselves (Gal 5:13–14). If we take Paul's statement seriously, do you think that your neighbor will notice? If time and money are involved, do you think that your spouse and

1 The Apostle Paul reinforces this point in Romans 13:9.

kids will notice?

The Ten Commandments remind us what love looks like from God's perspective, not ours. God created a community of individuals—not just you or me—in His image. If God created and loves my neighbor, perhaps I too can learn to love them. God's love means honor our parents; love means do not murder . . .

We need reminders; we need clear boundaries. In the Ten Commandments God graciously provides them both.

DAY 30: *The Ten Commandments*

"And God spoke all these words, saying, I am the Lord your God, who brought you out of the land of Egypt, out of the house of slavery" (Exod 20:1–2).

W hy, as Christians, do we need to know about the Ten Commandments? The short answer is because Jesus tells us to[1]. Reformer John Calvin reinforced this point and said that the law had three chief purposes: to teach us about God's will, to aid civil authorities, and to guide our daily lives (Haas 2006, 100).

Still, as postmodern people, we have contempt for law. We live undisciplined lives, ignore posted speed limits, and cheat on our taxes. We want to be independent and in control of our own lives. We do not want anyone, not even God, telling us what to do. The Ten Commandments remind us that we remain rebellious sons and daughters of Adam and Eve.

Our rebellion against God is called sin. Sin takes at least three forms: falling short of expectations (sin), breaking a law (transgression), and not doing something we should do (iniquity). I sin when I *try* to love God with all my heart, soul, and mind, but fail to do so consistently. I transgress the

1 *"For truly, I say to you, until heaven and earth pass away, not an iota, not a dot, will pass from the Law until all is accomplished" (Matt 5:18).*

law when I murder someone. I commit iniquity when I ignore (dishonor) my parents in their old age, leaving their care to my siblings when I am able to help but refuse to. Although these three words are used interchangeably, these distinctions remain helpful.

In our rebellion, the law comes as an act of grace pointing us the way back to God. The Ten Commandments can be thought of as God's healthy boundaries for life in the Christian community and as an example to the world.

So what is helpful to know about the Ten Commandments?

The Bible tells us that God is the Lord of lords and uses covenants to define His relationship with us. A covenant is a treaty or agreement outlining the duties and obligations of the ruler to the ruled. The Bible outlines covenants with Adam, Noah, Abraham, Moses, and David and the New Covenant with Christ. The Ten Commandments are part of the covenant with Moses.

Jeremiah prophesied the coming of a new covenant that would be written on our hearts (Jer 31:30–31). Matthew's Gospel describes this new covenant with five explicit commandments given by Jesus: 5:17–20, 17:9, 19:16–21, 22:36–40,

28:18–20. Two of these have already been mentioned: obey the law (Matt 5:17–20) and the double love command (love God; love neighbor in Matt 22:36–40).

Why do Christians need to understand the Ten Commandments? The Ten Commandments help us to understand what it means to be God's people and to follow Christ's commandment to obey the law.

Almighty Father, beloved Son, Holy Spirit. Bless us so that we will take your laws into our hearts and follow them in our daily lives. May sin and evil not attract us. May our friends practice righteousness and may we follow their example. Guide us with songs of righteousness and holy prayers (Ps 1:1–2). Let us honor your holy boundaries and remove the sin from our lives. To you and you alone be the glory. Amen.

Questions

1. What is a covenant?

2 Who has God made covenants with?

3. Why should we pay attention to the Law of Moses?

4. What are two commandments under the new covenant?

DAY 31: No Other Gods (First Commandment)

"You *shall have no other gods before me.*"

(Exod 20:3; Deut 5:7)

Why does God claim exclusive right to our allegiance and forbid worship of other gods?

God's sovereignty over our lives arises from his role as creator. Did we do anything to earn our creation? No. Our first independent act after God created us was in fact to sin and rebel against God's only law—do not eat of the tree (Gen 2:17). Did we do anything to earn God's restoration and salvation? No—God himself paid the penalty of our sin in sending his son to die on a cross on our behalf.

God's permits only one path to salvation—through Jesus Christ. We cannot approach God on our own. Two reasons suggest why.

The first reason arises because of God's eternal nature—God stands outside of time. God's infinite nature implies that he can approach us, but we cannot approach him. Think of the problem of setting a meeting date with an eternal God—maybe God's convenient date is 30 AD or maybe 3000 AD. How exactly are we to show up or even arrange the date? The apostle Paul writes: "*For while we were still weak, at the right time Christ died for the ungodly." (Rom 5:6)*

The second reason arises because of God's Holy nature. Holy implies sacred or set apart. God is holy; we are not. God's holiness precludes us from approaching him on our own.

Because we cannot approach God on our own, either physically or morally, a hidden path to God outside of Christ logically does not exist. In fact, the idea that a hidden path to God exists ignores both of the above problems and focuses on three misconceptions about God's holiness.

The first misconception argues that we are basically good and can approach God without divine intervention. If we were basically good, then God's holiness would pose no problem. Christ's sacrifice on the cross would be unnecessary and keeping the Law of Moses would be theoretically possible. Unfortunately, after Adam and Eve *bad* seed (original sin) ran in the family.

The second misconception argues that God himself is not good, which is obviously not true. As the ultimate sovereign, God is the ultimate lawmaker and defines what is good and what is not. It is not an accident that God declares creation to be good seven times in the creation account[1]. God declares creation good because he created and sustains it. Because our

1 Genesis 1 verses 4, 10, 12, 18, 21, 25, and 31.

lives depend on both God's creation of and provision for our universe, God must be good!

The third misconception presumes ignorance of God's holiness. As the apostle Paul told the Athenians:

> *The times of ignorance God overlooked, but now he*
> *commands all people everywhere to repent, because*
> *he has fixed a day on which he will judge the world in*
> *righteousness by a man whom he has appointed; and of*
> *this he has given assurance to all by raising him from*
> *the dead. (Acts 17:30–31)*

In view of modern communication systems, the Gospel message is close to reaching the entire human race—even people groups unknown to Paul's generation. The ignorance argument is accordingly less credible today than in Paul's time.

God deserves our worship. The first commandment in the law requires it.

Heavenly Father, *"how majestic is your name in all the earth! You have set your glory above the heavens. Out of the mouth of babies and infants, you have established strength because of your foes, to still the enemy and the avenger." (Ps 8:1–2)* May we praise your name forever. In the name of the Father, the Son, and the Holy

Spirit, Amen.

Questions

1.   What is the first commandment?

2.   What makes God sovereign?

3.   What are two reasons why no unknown path to God exists?

4.   What three misconceptions about God's holiness prevent us from seeing the exclusive need for Christ?

DAY 32: No Images (Second Commandment)

You shall not make for yourself a carved image, or any likeness of anything that is in heaven above, or that is in the earth beneath, or that is in the water under the earth. You shall not bow down to them or serve them, for I the LORD your God am a jealous God, visiting the iniquity of the fathers on the children to the third and the fourth generation of those who hate me, but showing steadfast love to thousands of those who love me and keep my commandments. (Exod 20:4–6; Deut 5:8–10)

*D*id you ever wait until the second time your mother called (as if her intent were unclear) before responding? Why? Repetition implies emphasis. In Hebrew poetry we see a special kind of repetition where the first and second sentences say the same thing just in different words. A good example of a Hebrew doublet is found in Psalm 115, where we read:

> *Our God is in the heavens; he does all that he pleases. Their idols are silver and gold, the work of human hands. They have mouths, but do not speak; eyes, but do not see. (Ps 115:3–5)*

The comparison is between God, who is alive (lives in heaven; does what he pleases), and idols, which are not alive (made of metal by humans; have silent mouths and useless eyes).

The problem of idol worship runs deep in the human psyche. An idol is anything that we treat as more important than God. And we have many such things—family members, friends, work, school, political leaders, pop stars, sports heroes, philosophies, bank accounts, insurance policies, health plans— the list is endless.

Louie Giglio (2003, 113), a Christian musician, says that if you want a list of the idols in your life, ask where you spend your money, your time, your energy, and your loyalty. Check out your priorities and you will find the idols that threaten your faith, your mental health, and, perhaps, your life.

The second commandment is not about God's vanity. When we put our faith in idols, we set ourselves up for a hard fall. All idols eventually break and, when they do, we break with them. The outcome of our brokenness often results in depression, addiction, or suicide; collectively, it results in oppression, injustice, and war.

The obsession in our society with work and "having it all", for example, leads us to abuse our own health and to undervalue anyone who does not work. Instead of valuing time with our family, we refuse to use our vacation leave and we return to work even before we have to. Instead of relaxing or exercising when we are off from work, we bring work home and make poor food choices. Instead of seeing our young people and senior citizens as created in the image of God, we see them as "dependents" who do not work. It is not surprising, therefore, that they develop self-image problems and depression, or worse; substitutes for the living God's role in our life are cheap imitations.

Almighty God, Great I AM (Exod 3:14). You created us in your image; you have imbued us with your beauty. Shelter our hearts and minds from idols that ensnare us stealing the dignity and protection of your divine image. Help us to keep your image sacred and holy. Keep our faith strong in the power of your Holy Spirit. In Jesus' name, Amen.

Questions

1. What is an idol?

2. What happens when our idols prove false?

3. What role does repetition play in interpreting scripture?

DAY 33: Honor The Name (Third Commandment)

"You shall not take the name of the LORD your God in vain, for the LORD will not hold him guiltless who takes his name in vain." (Exod 20:7; Deut 5:11)

Years ago when I studied in Germany, I had a friend from Belgium who was known only by his last name. When I asked around, not even the department secretary knew his first name. His first name was reserved for family and no one else.

God is also sensitive about his name and how it is used (Ezek 36:20-23).

In Old Testament Hebrew, numerous names for God are given. God's covenantal name, YHWH, which God gave to Moses from the burning bush (Exod 3:14), is sacred for Jews. When Jews encounter YHWH in scripture, they normally substitute Adonai, which means Lord. Most translators honor this tradition. By contrast, the generic name for God in Hebrew is Elohim which is, for example, the word for God used in Genesis 1:1.

The treatment of God's name is an extension of the holiness of God. Holy means both being set apart and the idea of sacredness. The Tabernacle, and later the Temple in Jerusalem, was constructed to observe three levels of increasing holiness: the courtyard for Jews, the Holy Place for priests, and the Holy of Holies for the high priest—but only on the Day of Atonement (Exod 30:10). The Ark of the Covenant resided in the Holy of Holies.

Although the Jewish sacrifice system ended with the destruction of the temple in AD 70, God's name is still holy. The Apostle Paul, for example, wrote:

And *being found in human form, he humbled himself by becoming obedient to the point of death, even death on a cross. Therefore God has highly exalted him and bestowed on him the* NAME *that is above every name, so that at the* NAME *of Jesus every knee should bow, in heaven and on earth and under the earth, and every tongue confess that Jesus Christ is Lord, to the glory of God the Father. (Phil 2:8–11)*

Therefore, the commandment *not* to profane the name of God is one to be taken seriously. The author of Proverbs writes: *"The fear of the LORD is the beginning of knowledge." (Prov 1:7)* We honor God by refraining from vulgar language and refusing to make empty promises leveraged on God's name.

But honoring God's name is more than merely not us-

ing bad language. Our conduct should bring honor to God—
our actions must be consistent with the faith we profess (Jas
2:17).

One of the greatest rewards in heaven is simply to bear
the NAME (Rev 22:4). Why not start now?

Almighty God, may our words and our actions reflect your
glory and bring honor to your name, this day and every day. In
the power of your Holy Spirit, cleanse our thoughts; sanctify
our hearts; and redeem our actions that we may be a blessing to
those around us. In Jesus' name, Amen.

Questions

1. What names of God does the Bible use?

2. What does holy mean? How does the organization of the
temple in Jerusalem reflect the holiness of God?

3. Does the New Testament continue to honor the name of
God? In what ways?

4. How will we be honored in heaven?

DAY 34: Keep The Sabbath Holy (Fourth Commandment)

Observe the Sabbath day, to keep it holy, as the LORD your God commanded you. Six days you shall labor and do all your work, but the seventh day is a Sabbath to the LORD your God. On it you shall not do any work, you or your son or your daughter or your male servant or your female servant, or your ox or your donkey or any of your livestock, or the sojourner who is within your gates, that your male servant and your female servant may rest as well as you. You shall remember that you were a slave in the land of Egypt, and the LORD your God brought you out from there with a mighty hand and an outstretched arm. Therefore the LORD your God commanded you to keep the Sabbath day. (Deut 5:12–15)

The divine origin of the Sabbath is well-attested in both the Old and New Testaments. In the Old Testament, it is the only commandment that appears also in the creation account and it is also the longest commandment—an indicator of emphasis. In the New Testament, Jesus refers to himself as the Lord of the Sabbath (Matt 12:8; Luke 6:5) and performs several miracles specifically on the Sabbath. Why all this attention to the Sabbath?

A key to understanding Sabbath is found in Hebrews 4, which list four aspects of Sabbath rest: physical rest, weekly Sabbath rest, rest in the Promised Land, and heavenly rest—our return to the Garden of Eden.

Physical rest is underrated by many Christians. Jesus says: *"Come to me, all who labor and are heavy laden, and I will give you rest."* *(Matt 11:28)* How are we to love God and love our neighbors when we are physically exhausted all the time? Sabbath rest allows us to build the physical, emotional, and spiritual capacity to experience God and to have compassion for our neighbors.

We see a clue to this interpretation of Sabbath when we compare the Exodus and Deuteronomy renderings of the Fourth Commandment. Deuteronomy adds the sentence: *"You shall remember that you were a slave in the land of Egypt, and the LORD your God brought you out from there with a mighty hand and an outstretched arm."* *(Deut 5:15)* Free people rest; slaves work. Are we, Americans, truly free? Sabbath rest is a symbol of our Christian freedom.

The Promised Land, promised rest (Ps 95:11), heaven, and the new Eden (Rev 22:2) all display and reinforce Sabbath imagery. The image of our Divine Shepherd is one who gives heavenly rest: *"He makes me lie down in green pastures. He leads me beside still waters." (Ps 23:2)* Sadly, this image of rest only seems to come up at funerals. Why not start now?

Compassionate Father, Lover of our souls, Holy Spirit. Draw us to yourself: Open our hearts; Illumine our thoughts; Strengthen our hands in your service. Grant us rest with you today and every day. In Jesus' name, Amen.

Questions

1. How is Sabbath rest a divinely ordained practice in scripture?

2. What are the four aspects of rest outlined in Hebrews 4?

3. Why is Sabbath rest a key to our spirituality?

4. How are rest and freedom linked?

DAY35: *Honor Your Parents (Fifth Commandment)*

"Honor your father and your mother, as the LORD your God commanded you, that your days may be long, and that it may go well with you in the land that the LORD your God is giving you." (Deut 5:16)[1]

Who do you honor? Who do you honor most?

As postmodern Americans, we love the language of individual autonomy and freedom. Our laws limit the rights of almost all authority figures—parents, teachers, supervisors, police, politicians, even pastors.

Honoring one's parents and the general use of father-son language of the Bible was common terminology in the Ancient Near East. For example, being created in the image of God implies a father-son (or father-daughter) relationship, which also appears when Adam fathers Seth in his image[2]. It also appears in the Lord's Prayer, for example, in the phrase: "*on earth as it is in heaven.*" *(Matt 6:10)* The idea in the covenant with Moses, therefore, is that God is our suzerain (literally: King of kings or

---

1 Also Exod 20:12; Matt 15:4; Mark 7:10.

2 e.g. Genesis 1:27 and 5:3. Meredith Kline (2006, 62) writes: "*And knowledge of what one's Father-God is, is knowledge of what, in creaturely semblance, one must be himself.*"

Father king)[3] and we are his vassals (subordinate kings)[4]. Vassals honor suzerains as children should honor their parents.

Oh well and good, you say, but why must we honor our parents?

The apostle Paul described the fifth commandment as the only one that includes a promise: *that it may go well with you and that you may live long in the land.*[5] This promise implies that we do not always know what is best for us ourselves.

The apostle Paul redefined hierarchy. He wrote: children obey your parents; parents do not upset your children. Likewise, he redefined other relationships. Wives respect your husbands; husbands love your wives like yourself. Slaves respect your masters; masters treat your slaves as family (Eph 6:1–9). Paul later required elders in the church to manifest these new relationships (1 Tim 3:4). The principle here is: *"Whatever you*

---

3 Today most governments are not governed by kings so we use less personal language. Today, we talk about superpowers and client states. However, the concept is the same.

4 We know this, in part, because the Ten Commandments were written on two stone tablets (Exod 24:12; Deut 5:22). In Hittite treaties, two tablets were routinely recorded, one for the suzerain and one for the vassal. Sometime people speculate that the first four commandments dealing with our relationship with God were on the first tablet while the last six commandments dealing with our relationship with our neighbors were written on the second tablet, as in the Heidelberg Catechism (PCUSA 1999, 4.093). It is more likely, however, that the first and second tablets were identical. These treaties were written on durable materials, such as stone, to prevent fraud (Kline (1963, 19).

5 Deut 5:16; Eph 6:2–3.

do, work heartily, as for the Lord and not for men [or women]." (Col 3:23)

If Christ is Lord of our lives, then hierarchy takes on new meaning. Two-way secular relationships are transformed into three-way relationships under God: every relationship is you, me, and God. Marriage transforms from a contract (two-way) into a covenant (three-way). Relationships morph from social transactions into opportunities to display Christ's love for one another.

Jesus says: *"Behold, I am making all things new."* (Rev 21:5) Transformed relationships allow the kingdom of God to break into a fallen world here and now.

Almighty Father. King of kings. Lord of lords. Thank you for your ongoing presence in our lives. Redeem our relationships; guarantee our fidelity; mentor our leadership. In the power of your Holy Spirit, bless our families, our churches, and our work places. In Jesus' precious name, Amen.

Questions

1. Why should we obey the Fifth Commandment?

2. How did the apostle Paul redefine the nature of authority

in relationships?

3.   What is a three-way relationship? How might it differ from a two-way relationship?

DAY 36: *Do Not murder (Sixth Commandment)*

"You shall not murder." (Exod 20:13)

T he Sixth Commandment—you shall not murder—seems cut and dry. In case you missed it, the Bible repeats it five times using the exact same words[1]. The punishment for murder—death—is given in the account of Noah (Gen 9:11).

When Jesus talks about murder, he compares it with being angry with and insulting your brother or sister. He then makes a curious comment: [if] *"your brother has something against you, leave your gift there before the altar and go. First be reconciled to your brother, and then come and offer your gift."* *(Matt 5:24)* This comment is curious for two reasons. First, at the time when he spoke only priests were allowed to enter the Holy Place in the Temple and approach the altar. Second, this comment appears to make reconciliation with our brother or sister more important than reconciliation with God.

So what is that all about? Jesus is reminding his listeners not of the Temple, but of the first murder story in the Bible— the story of Cain and Abel. He uses it as an object lesson. Cain got angry with his brother, Abel, after Abel brought a better sacrifice to God. For this, Cain murdered Abel (Gen 4:1–8). The

---

1 Also: Deut 5:17; Matt 5:21; 19:18; Rom 13:9.

lesson is that we should reconcile with each other before anger gets out of control and before we do something that we may later regret (Matt 5:23–24).

Jesus is making two important points.

First, Jesus teaches us to prevent murder by removing the incentive to murder. This lesson can then be applied to all sorts of situations, not just murder.

Second, asking God for forgiveness (bringing a gift) does not erase the sin that we have committed against one another. If we murder someone, asking God's forgiveness does not restore the life lost or heal the emotional devastation experienced by the victim's family. Forgiveness cannot be just about words.

The point is that asking God for forgiveness, such as repeating a prayer of confession on Sunday morning, neither requires a change of attitude towards our sin (Jesus' first point) nor compensating those hurt by what we have done (Jesus' second point). True repentance (a real change in heart) answers the first point; making restitution (compensating our victims) answers the second point.

Does Jesus' lesson mean that we should never be angry? No. Anger has an object. Some objects of our anger are selfish and evil; some are not.

Jesus clearly got angry about injustice, about those doing business in the temple (John 2: 14–17), and about the hard-hearted Pharisees that refused to allow good works, such as healing, on the Sabbath. By contrast, the Pharisees got so angry at Jesus' healing on the Sabbath (because it made them look bad) that they responded by plotting his death (Matt 12:10–14).

Compassionate Father, beloved Son, ever-present Spirit. Thank you giving us healthy boundaries in your law. Cleanse our hearts of jealousy, envy, and other evil passions that lead us to sin. In Jesus' name, Amen.

Questions

1.   How many times is the Sixth Commandment repeated in the Bible?

2.   What story does Jesus use to teach about murder?

3.   What are the two lessons that Jesus teaches?

4.   What do these lessons teach about forgiveness?

5.   When is anger forbidden; when is it okay?

DAY 37: Do Not Commit Adultery (Seventh Commandment)

"And you shall not commit adultery." (Exod 20:14)[1]

*A*t the heart of adultery is almost always a lie. The lie is that our private lives are and should remain private. The truth, however, is that our actions always affect those around us.

Ask King David. He thought that he could have a quiet affair with Bathsheba. When she got pregnant, he tried to hush it up first by calling her husband, Uriah the Hittite, back from service in the army to the palace. The idea was that if Uriah slept with his wife, David's sin would be covered up. Uriah spoiled this plan by remaining loyal to David and refusing to return home. Unable to cover up his sin, David sent word to Uriah's commander to place him on the front line in battle and then abandon him to the Amorites. Uriah died in battle (2 Sam 11). Pretty soon everyone heard about David's sin and attempted cover up. Psalm 30 records David's distress over his sin. Psalm 51 records David's confession to God. God forgave David but David's sin led to the death of his child (2 Sam 12:13–14).

Adultery, divorce, and other forms of immorality are the

---

1 Also: Deut 5:18; Matt 5:27; 19:18; Rom 13:9.

consequence of yielding to forbidden desires and temptations that threaten to destroy healthy relationships[1] and tear apart our families. They also stand in contrast to God's intent for human marriage, which is life-long marriage between one man and one woman.

Marriage is not just a romantic idea. If we view our relationships as simply serving our own needs, our children lose out. According to the U.S. Census (2011, 68), the share of children born to unwed mothers rose from 27 percent in 1990 to 40 percent in 2007. This one statistic implies that the prospects for children in America have plummeted in our generation. Think more poverty. Think more drug use. Think more suicide. Marriage is not just a romantic idea.

Jesus deplored divorce, permitting it only in the case of sexual immorality, and relating it to adultery[2]. The covenant of marriage (Mal 2:14) involves for us two parts: both a covenantal sign (physical intimacy) and a covenantal oath (the marriage promise)[3]. Sexual immorality breaks the first part, but not nec-

---

1 My first ministry experience as a young adult arose when my pastor and mentor encouraged me to start a summer youth program. The program was a success and I continued this ministry until I was married some years later. My mentor, however, was discovered by a church member to be having a homosexual affair. The affair cost him his pastorate and his marriage; it cost me an important mentor; and it cost the church a talented pastor.

2 Matt 5:32; 19:9.

3 For Adam, we see Adam's rib being taken out to create Eve (a kind of cut-

essarily the second.

Jesus' teaching about adultery parallels his teaching about murder. Lust leads to immorality so Jesus cautions us to avoid lust and thereby prevent adultery. He then interrupts this discussion of adultery to launch into a bit of hyperbole: *"If your right eye causes you to sin, tear it out . . . And if your right hand causes you to sin, cut it off and throw it away." (Matt 5:29–30)* After this aside, he returns to his discussion of adultery. The implication is that the body part in view is not an eye or a hand but something a bit more personal! Jesus clearly deplores divorce and immorality.

Almighty God. We praise you for loving our families and caring for our children. Guard our hearts and minds. Chasten us to be faithful to our spouses. In the power of your Holy Spirit, keep us mindful of your will for our lives. In Jesus' precious name, Amen.

Questions

1. Why is adultery associated with lies? What is the biggest lie?

---

ting ceremony) and an oath—*"she is bone of my bones."* (Hugenberger 1994, 342–43; Gen 2:21–23)

2. What was the story of David and Bathsheba? What was the consequence of David's sin?

3. Why is adultery wrong from God's perspective? How is wrong from our perspective?

4. What did Jesus have to say about divorce?

5. How is adultery like murder?

6. What is the real focus of Jesus' hyperbole?

DAY 38: Do Not Steal (Eighth Commandment)

"And you shall not steal." (Exod 20:15)[1]

The story of the rich young ruler seems to bother Americans more than other biblical stories, most likely, because we are a wealthy nation. The story is found in all three of the synoptic Gospels. The story begins when the man asks: *"What must I do to inherit eternal life?"* Jesus responds by listing off the commandments having to do with loving our neighbors. The man responds saying: *"All these [commandments] I have kept from my youth"*—is there anything further I must do? Jesus replied: *"Sell all that you have and give to the poor, . . . and come, follow me."* At this point, the man went away sad unwilling to respond to Jesus' invitation (paraphrase)[2].

What does this have to do with not stealing?

Avoiding evil is not the same thing as being good. It is presumably less tempting to steal if you are wealthy than if you are poor. If you are wealthy and motivated by greed, you can delegate little acts of theft to subordinates or convince legislators to change the law to make little acts of theft legal. The rich young ruler no doubt truthfully answered Jesus' question about

---

1 Also: Lev 19:11; Deut 5:19; Matt 19:18; Rom 13:9.
2 Matt 19; Mark 10; Luke 18.

the commandments.

However, what if the rich young ruler were a subprime lender and came to Jesus, what do you think he might say? Is it stealing to sell a mortgage to a poor person who probably cannot repay the loan? What if the probability of repayment is reduced by one percent? What about five percent? Before the 2007 financial crisis regulations were amended to make subprime lending easier. Was it enough to have complied with such regulations? What if you worked for the government?

Taking positive steps to be good is not easy.

The apostle Paul makes this distinction when he lists works of the flesh (vices) and lists of fruits of the spirit (virtues). He writes:

> Now the works of the flesh are evident: sexual immoral-ity, impurity, sensuality, idolatry, sorcery, enmity, strife, jealousy, fits of anger, rivalries, dissensions, divisions, envy, drunkenness, orgies, and things like these. I warn you, as I warned you before, that those who do such things will not inherit the kingdom of God. But the fruit of the Spirit is love, joy, peace, patience, kindness, goodness, faithfulness, gentleness, self-control; against

such things there is no law. (Gal 5:19–23)

Paul's list does not include stealing, but we all know which list that one belongs to!

It is interesting that in the Sermon on Mount Jesus does not talk specifically about theft the way he does about murder and adultery. In some sense, he did not need to. If greed leads to cheating one's neighbor, then obviously we should avoid being greedy in order to prevent cheating. Better yet, why not practice generosity?

Gracious God. Thank you for lavishing your love and generosity on us. Grant us generous hearts and helping hands that we might reflect your image. May our security be in You, not our possessions. In the name of the Father, the Son, and Holy Spirit, Amen.

Questions

1.   What question did the rich young ruler pose to Jesus and how did he respond? Why do we care?

2.   Does greed lead to theft? Why or why not?

3.   If you are wealthy, why is it easier not to steal than it is to be generous?

DAY 39: Do Not Lie (Ninth Commandment)

"And you shall not bear false witness against your neighbor."
(Exod 20:16)

The opposite of a lie is the truth.

We worship the God of truth. From the burning bush, God tells Moses that his name is: *"I AM WHO I AM."* *(Exod 3:14)* Moses believed in God; Pharaoh refused to. When God presented the truth of his own existence, the nation of Israel was born. It is, accordingly, not surprising that the God of truth commands his people not to lie!

Bearing false witness is, however, more than an untruth; it is a deliberate deception with a specific objective. The exposition in Exodus 23:1–3 outline three specific issues: spreading a false report, perverting justice in court, and giving biased testimony. Spreading a false report could be simple gossip or it could be committing libel. Perverting justice can, of course, be done in many ways. Being biased out can be motivated by poverty or various affinities (family ties, race, language, social class, national origin, creed, or even locality).

These prejudices and injustices are so common that we are more often surprised by integrity than by bias. The recent debate over the death penalty, for example, hangs less on a dispute over the penalty than on the disbelief that justice will occur. Is it any wonder that Pilate, a corrupt official himself, would ask Jesus: *"What is truth?" (John 18:38)*

The story of the woman caught in adultery is probably the most celebrated capital judgment case in scripture. The woman's guilt is not in question; the only question was the penalty. The Pharisees asked Jesus: *"Now in the Law Moses commanded us to stone such women. So what do you say?" (John 8:5)*

Notice that under Jewish law both parties in adultery face the same penalty of death (Lev 20:10). Because the Pharisee covered up the man's identity, they broke the Ninth Commandment in presenting this case. In other words, they offered biased testimony and did not seek true justice.

Jesus points to the Pharisee' bias when he says: *"Let him who is without sin among you be the first to throw a stone at her."* *(John 8:7)* The law required that witnesses to the crime throw the first stone (Deut 17:7). If anyone picks up a stone, then that person is liable for prosecution under the law because they have not revealed the identity of the man who participated in the adultery. And, the penalty for perjury was the same penalty as for the alleged crime (Deut 19:18–19). The Pharisees understand their dilemma and they leave.

Jesus' words to the woman are important. He says: *"'Has no one condemned you?' She said, 'No one, Lord.' And Jesus said, 'Neither do I condemn you; go, and from now on sin no more.'" (John 8:10–11)* Jesus offers both truth and grace. Truth or grace, by themselves, is not the Gospel. Truth alone is too harsh to be heard; grace alone ignores the law. Jesus seeks our transformation, not our conviction under law (Rom 12:2).

Almighty God, gracious savior, spirit of truth. We praise you for being the way, the truth, and the life (John 14:6). Grant us a discerning spirit to know the truth and a gracious spirit for sharing it. To you and you alone be the glory. In Jesus' name, Amen.

Questions

1. Why is God often referred to as the spirit of truth?

2. What types of false witnesses does scripture talk about?

3. Why is the death penalty hard to apply?

4. What lessons can be learned from the story of the woman caught in adultery?

5. Why did he ask those without sin to cast the first stone?

DAY 40: Do Not Covet (Tenth Commandment)

And you shall not covet your neighbor's wife. And you shall not desire your neighbor's house, his field, or his male servant, or his female servant, his ox, or his donkey, or anything that is your neighbor's. (Deut 5:21)[1]

*H*ow many marriages and families have been destroyed over the years by the love of money? Disagreements over money are often cited as a leading cause of divorce.

Covetness is a cross between greed and envy. Greed is an extreme desire to possess something, while envy is an extreme desire that someone else not possess that which we desire. In either case, our desires lead us to treat others badly.

Both greed and envy are among the seven deadly (moral) sins popularized by Thomas Aquinas in the twelfth century. Aquinas listed these as pride (vainglory), envy, anger, sloth (spiritual apathy), greed, gluttony, and lust[2]. He described them as capital sins because they lead to other sins and are the opposite of particular virtues (Aquinas 2003, 317–20). Just as virtue is an ongoing good character trait, a vice is an ongoing bad character trait.

Jesus coined a new word for covetness (mammon)

---

1 Also: Exod 20:17; Deut 7:25; Rom 7:7; 13:9.

2 The seven deadly sin are often described using their Latin names. Those are superbia (pride), invidia (envy), ira (anger), gula (gluttony), luxuria (lust), avarita (greed), and accidia (sloth) (Fairlie, 2006, iv).

when he said: "*Ye cannot serve God and mammon.*"[1] The King James Version (KJV) of the Bible transliterates the Greek word, mammon, which may also be translated as the god of money. The apostle Paul preferred to refer to covetness as the love of money. For example, Paul wrote:

> *For the love of money is a root of all kinds of evil.*
> *Some people, eager for money, have wandered from*
> *the faith and pierced themselves with many griefs. (1*
> *Tim 6:10 NIV)*

While covetness is a vice that causes relational difficulties, mammon is also idolatry. Something becomes idolatrous—becomes a god—when we love it more than God. Jesus warns us:

> *No one can serve two masters, for either he will hate*
> *the one and love the other, or he will be devoted to the*
> *one and despise the other. (Matt 6:24)*

Here we enter the realm of obsession and addiction as slaves of sin (John 8:34). We can be addicted to almost anything. Gerald May (1988, 14) writes: "*addiction is a state of compulsion, obsession, or preoccupation that enslaves a person's will and desire.*" Two tests can be applied to potentially addictive behavior. Does the behavior disrupt relationships with the people closest to you? Do you experience withdrawal symp-

1 Luke 16:13 KJV; Matt 6:24 KJV.

toms when you give it up? In this context, do you think covetness can rise to the level of addiction?

Henry Cloud (2008, 154) has an interesting suggestion for dealing with pain: *"Look at the misery and then make a personal rule that will keep it from happening."* In this case, God has seen the pain in our lives and has given us a rule: don't covet.

More generally, the Ten Commandments do three things: they reduce our pain, they simplify our lives, and they help us to model ourselves after the One who we claim to follow.

Loving Father. You clothe the birds that neither spin or reap (Matt 6:26). You send the rain and the sunshine on the just and the unjust without discrimination (Matt 5:45). You make the day and the night to bless us with activities and with sleep (Gen 1:5). We cast our obsessions and addictions at your feet. In the power of your Holy Spirit, heal our relationships and soften our hearts that we might grow more like you with each passing day. In Jesus's name, Amen.

Questions

1.   How would you describe covetness?

2. What is the difference between greed and envy?

3. Name the seven deadly sins.

4. What is mammon? Who coined the term?

5. What are two tests for addictive behavior?

6. How can boundaries be established to limit misery?

7. What are three things that the Ten Commandments do for us?

SPIRITUAL DISCIPLINES

Why is Music an important Spiritual Discipline?

Why Practice Daily Devotions?

Why Exercise?

Why is Work a Spiritual Discipline?

What is Spiritual about Marriage and Family?

Why Participate in a Small Group?

Why does Sabbath Rest keep coming up?

What exactly is Worship?

Spiritual disciplines help us answer the question: How DO WE KNOW? Because we can neither build a physical tower nor a metaphorical tower to God, especially since Pentecost[1] God himself in His Holy Spirit has worked with us in the spiritual disciplines to answer this question. This is sometimes referred to as the process of sanctification[2].

Spiritual disciplines may serve at least three objectives. One objective is to help remove impediments that affect our relationship with God—things like sin. Another objective is to respond to a special path of grace that God has uniquely given us. A further objective is to facilitate the process of reconciliation with those we have sinned against.

Contemplative prayer focuses on reducing impediments to our relationship with God. For example, Foster (1992, 161–164) sees three steps in contemplative prayer: recollection (concentrating our minds to become fully present), quieting our spirits, and spiritual ecstasy—God's response.

By contrast, Thomas (2010, 7, 83, 211) sees nine spiritual personality types that lead us to God's grace. These are: naturalists, sensates, traditionalists, ascetics, activists, caregivers,

---

1 The story of the Tower of Babel is found in Genesis 11:1-9. The story of Pentecost is found in Acts 2:1-4.

2 The Apostle Paul writes about his own struggle with sanctification in Philippians 3:7-11.

enthusiasts, contemplatives, and intellectuals. For example, the traditionalist experiences God through three main elements: ritual, symbol, and sacrifice. By contrast, for intellectuals, the sermon is not just part of worship—it is worship.

The process of reconciliation is seldom addressed as a separate spiritual discipline, but needs to factor into many disciplines and may even be part of church governance. We see it addressed, in part, in Christian service, in work relationships, our marriages, our small groups, and our worship. If the spiritual disciplines are ranked in order of need, reconciliation would clearly rank near the top of the list.

For Presbyterians, church goverance stresses reconciliation through group decision-making. Almost every decision in church life requires committee approval and oversight. By building reconciliation into basic decision-making processes, the need to practice a specific spiritual discipline is, accordingly, minimized. However, when special problems arise, reconciliation may be a separately highlighted process, sometimes referred to as peacemaking[3].

---

3 The Apostle Paul writes: *"If possible, so far as it depends on you, live peaceably with all." (Rom 12:18) Sande (2004, 22)* lists 6 peacemaking responses to conflict including: 1. overlook the offense; 2. reconcile the parties; 3. negotiate, 4. mediate, or 5. arbitrate to resolve the conflict; and 6. hold people accountable for their actions.

DAY 41: Why is music an important spiritual discipline?

Then Moses and the people of Israel sang this song to the LORD, saying, "I will sing to the LORD, for he has triumphed gloriously; the horse and his rider he has thrown into the sea." (Exod 15:1)

Why does scripture's account of salvation history often sound like a music video? One reason is that they mark important transitions in the narrative of scripture. Songs of praise accompany, for example, both the salvation of Israel from the Egyptians after crossing the Red Sea, and their entrance into the Promised Land[1]. Hannah's song marks the birth of the prophet, Samuel, (1 Sam 2:1–10). Songs also begin and end the New Testament: Mary's song marks her pregnancy (Luke 1:46–45); angels announce the birth of the baby Jesus with heavenly praise (Luke 2:14); and, of course, the songs of praise in the Book of Revelation remind us of Christ's second coming and eternal reign (e.g. Rev 19:5–8).

Music is special as a spiritual discipline because it helps unite our hearts and minds[2], and uniquely expresses Christian joy. God has sovereignly created and saved us. We respond in

1 Exod 15:1–21; Deut 32:1–43.
2 Dietrick Bonhoeffer once reportedly told his students (all good German intellectuals): *"If you want to be pastors, then you must sing Christmas carols!"* (Metaxas 2010, 129).

praise. Accordingly, our minds know that our debt is beyond repayment and our hearts rejoice from the depths of our being. We are loved by the King of kings and we want to tell the whole world! Words alone are not enough. Holy songs bind our hearts and minds together. Choral music is special, in particular, because it binds our hearts and minds in unity seldom seen elsewhere.

This unity of heart and mind in music is so complete that it does not allow us to choose one over the other[3]. Even instrumental music communicates complex forms and themes with deep emotion[4]. Because all of us have songs that we have memorized, music is a form of meditation practiced by virtually everyone. We repeat and memorize holy songs that then define who we are, who we were, and who we will be[5].

Holy music is a special gifting from God that draws our

---

3 Elliott (2006, 86) writes: *"Love is linked to knowledge. To love God you learn about him and rehearse his words constantly. This knowledge will fuel your emotions."*

4 Playing a musical score functions as a kind of subliminal message which reminds of song lyrics and touches different channels in our brains.

5 I caution my students to be careful about the music that they listen to: when Alzheimer's claims most of your mind, do you really want the last thing you remember to be the Oscar Mayer Wiener commercial or some heavy metal lyric?

hearts and minds to him.

Father God. We praise you with songs our whole life long. We serve you gladly and enter your presence with singing. We remember that you are God: you made us; we belong to you; we are your people—the sheep of one shepherd. We come to church with thanksgiving and trust your judgment. Your praise fills our hearts and we bless your name. For you are good and your love never fails us—even as we, ourselves, pass away (Ps 100). In the name of the Father, Son, and Holy Spirit, Amen.

Questions

1. What is common to all significant events in salvation history?

2. What two elements combine in music?

3. What is special about choral music?

4. What is a spiritual discipline? What are some objectives that spiritual disciplines serve?

5. Why is music like meditation?

DAY 42: Why devote time to daily prayer?

And the whole city was gathered together at the door. And he healed many who were sick with various diseases, and cast out many demons . . . And rising very early in the morning, while it was still dark, he departed and went out to a desolate place, and there he prayed. (Mark 1:33–35)

Jesus modeled daily prayer.

The Gospel of Luke records the most instances in which Jesus prays. The first instance of prayer is during his baptism when Jesus was anointed by the Holy Spirit in the form of a dove (Luke 3:21–22). When crowds gathered following miracles of healing, Jesus would retreat to a desolate place to pray (Luke 5:15). When the Pharisee attacked him for healing on the Sabbath, Jesus climbed a mountain and prayed all night—the following day, in what was among the most important decisions in his ministry, he chose the twelve apostles (Luke 6:12). Jesus, while praying alone among the disciples, posed the question: *"who do the crowds say that I am?" (Luke 9:18)* While praying with Peter, John, and James on a mountain top, Jesus was transfigured (Luke 9:28). Jesus was praying when the disciples asked him: *"Lord, teach us to pray." (Luke 11:1)* On the night before his death, Jesus prayed in the Garden of Gethsemane (Luke 22:41).

Two things that Jesus' prayers have in common in the Gospel of Luke are that he often prayed alone and he always prayed at critical points in his ministry. Significantly, God was visibly or audibly present in two of the seven incidences of Jesus' prayers recorded in Luke. In the Book of Acts, Peter and Paul are likewise both shown practicing the habit of prayer and experiencing important visions during prayer[1]. From these few examples, we know that God answers prayer.

Jesus is not our only model for prayer. Our first model of prayer arises in the book of Genesis. God appears to the pagan king, Abimelech, in a dream where God instructs him to return Sarah to Abraham and to ask Abraham to pray for his healing. Abimelech obeys God's instructions. Abraham then intercedes for Abimelech in prayer and God heals him (Gen 20:7, 17). Clearly, God cares for pagans and asks us, like Abraham, to pray for them. And, this is the first prayer in scripture!

Prayer is important in the psalms. For example, Psalm 51 is a prayer of confession. King David begs God's forgiveness following his adulterous affair with Bathsheba and the murder of her husband, Uriah the Hittite (2 Sam 11). Psalm 51 is im-

---

1 For example, Acts 10:9 and 9:11.

portant for Christians[2] because Jesus descends from King David (Matt 1:6–17).

The Apostle Paul also models prayer by admonishing us to: *"pray without ceasing" (1 Thess 5:17)*. Unceasing prayer suggests that daily prayer is something of a misnomer. What we really mean by *daily prayer* is prayer in the morning, prayer during meals, and prayer before bed. Prayer while running, prayer while deliberating decisions, prayer while walking to work . . .

Prayer means opening ourselves to God. And, sometimes, even words are spoken.

Oh dear Lord. Thank you for answering prayer. Thank you for visions that bring comfort; for healings that relieve pain; and for your presence that instills peace in our lives. Grow my faith. In the power of your Holy Spirit, shape me in the image of your son. In Jesus' name, Amen.

Questions

1. Where and when was the first prayer that Luke records for

---

2 Ps 51 is also important for Jews because it is an example of willful sin not covered by sacrifices under the Mosaic covenant. Both David's adultery and his murder of Uriah were intentional. Under the law, only unintentional sin could be atoned with sacrifices.

Jesus?

2. Where and when did Jesus typically pray?

3. What were some important occasions for Jesus' prayers?

4. What was interesting about the first prayer recorded in scripture?

DAY 43: Why exercise?

Flee from sexual immorality. Every other sin a person commits is outside the body, but the sexually immoral person sins against his own body. Or do you not know that your body is a temple of the Holy Spirit within you, whom you have from God? You are not your own, for you were bought with a price. So glorify God in your body. (1 Cor 6:18–20)

W hich spiritual discipline should I focus on?

Sin distracts and separates us from God. The spiritual disciplines of highest value target sins to which we, as Americans, are especially vulnerable—sexual immorality and gluttony. Both are sins against the body.

Jesus is clear when he says that sin begins in the heart. On the question of adultery, he says: *"everyone who looks at a woman with lustful intent has already committed adultery with her in his heart." (Matt 5:28)* This statement is immediately followed by hyperbole about chopping off body parts that lead to sin[1]. This transition from heart to body is an example of how the body and mind are unified[2].

The best example of the unity of body and mind ap-

1 I wonder, which body part is really in view here?

2 Macchia (2012, 104) writes: *"Your personal rule of life is formatted an reflected in your . . . physical priorities (the care and training of your body, mind, and heart)."*

plied to spiritual disciplines is found in Henri Nouwen's book, *Reaching Out*. Nouwen describes our spiritual journey as a unity of three dimensions—reaching inward to ourselves; reaching outward to others; and reaching upwards to God. In ourselves, we move from being lonely to becoming content in solitude. In our relationships with others, we move from hostility to hospitality. In our relationship with God, we move from illusion to prayer (Nouwen 1975, 15). The paradox of this unity in three dimensions is that progress in one dimension makes progress in the others easier.

This linkage of spiritual progress in different dimensions is especially important in dealing with sins of the body. Sins against the body invariably involve mild to severe addictions—obsessive behaviors that we repeatedly engage in. When we allow ourselves our "little indulgences", they spread to other aspects of our life. Bad behaviors turn into bad habits that turn into bad lifestyles. Undertaking a "fast" in vulnerable areas of our lives can nip bad behaviors early in the process. Gerald May (1988, 177) writes: *"It all comes down to quitting it, not engaging in the next addictive behavior, not indulging in the next temptation."* Physical discipline, accordingly, works to cleanse the whole system.

Why exercise? The simple answer is because your body is the temple of God. We are under obligation to ourselves and to God to keep our temple clean. A more nuanced answer is that the physical disciplines grant us strength to discipline other, less obvious, areas of our lives. The body and the mind are inseparable—physical exercise is a kind of beach assault on our island of sin[1]. Beach assaults, like the one on Iwo Jima during the Second World War[2], are risky but the payoff is huge. It is strange irony that when we exercise we often exhibit less interest in food, alcohol, even tobacco because we are more relaxed and self-confident.

In clinical pastoral education we were taught to look for dissidence between words and the body language of patients that we visited. This disharmony between words and body language is, of course, a measure of truth. In like manner, the biblical paradigm of beauty is that the truth of an object matches its appearance[3]. Did I mention that body and mind are closely

---

1 Reynolds (2012), who writes almost exclusively on a biblical perspective on weight-loss, notes that the first sin in the Bible is a temptation involving food (Gen 3:1–6).

2 Japan is a family of islands. In February 1945, United States amphibious forces landed on the Japanese island of Iwo Jima and engaged the Japanese military in one of the bloodies battles during the war.

3 *"Our modern images feature surface and finish; Old Testament images present structure and character. Modern images are narrow and restrictive;*

bound together?

Almighty Father. We praise you for the gift of life. Walk with us on the beach in the morning. Run with us through peaceful cornfields in the night. Swim with us as we exercise bodies and minds. In the power of your Holy Spirit, transform us into your people. In Jesus' precious name, Amen.

Questions

1. What is sin? How does it aid us in choosing a spiritual discipline?

2. What are the two most difficult temptations facing Americans? What do they have in common?

3. Where does sin begin according to Jesus?

4. How does Henri Nouwen describe the unity of our spiritual lives? What are the three dimensions and movements? How are they connected?

5. How do addictions begin? How can we stop them?

6. Why is exercise a spiritual discipline?

---

theirs were broad and inclusive…For us beauty is primarily visual; their idea of beauty included sensations of light, color, sound, smell, and even taste" (Dyrness 2001, 81).

DAY 44: Why is work a spiritual discipline?

"Whatever you do, work heartily, as for the Lord and not for men, knowing that from the Lord you will receive the inheritance as your reward." (Col 3:23–24)

The gravity of idolatrous sin is obvious. If our loyalty, time, energy, and money point to what we really worship (Giglio 2003, 113), then the heart of idolatrous activity has to be our work—inside or outside the church; inside or outside the home. Work is often also a source of stress, fear, and anxiety.

Jesus understands. At one point, he presented a word picture of lilies and kings. Then, he advised: *"do not seek what you are to eat and what you are to drink, nor be worried . . . Instead, seek his kingdom, and these things will be added to you." (Luke 12:27–31)* In other words, work is important; the kingdom of God is more important.

Work, as designed by God, is endowed with dignity. The Bible opens with God working—he creates (Welchel 2012, 7). God's only son did manual labor! If Christ worked first with his hands as a carpenter, then working with our hands also has honor. Most of the disciples worked as fishermen—do you think they came home smelling like lilies? One of Jesus' most radical acts was table ministry—he ate and drank with people who worked for a living (Matt 11:19)[1].

The Apostle Paul's attitude concerning work is significant in two ways. First, our work for human supervisors is also work for God! (Col 3:23–24). Second, many of the people that we work with and for are brothers and sisters—family—in Christ. How can anyone disrespect family? (Phlm 1:16). Impossible! Unthinkable!

One of the church's most important spiritual writers was a disabled veteran who worked in a kitchen. He hardly wrote anything at all. But he committed his work during the day to God in prayer. Brother Lawrence (1982, 23) wrote: *"We should offer our work to Him before we begin and thank Him afterwards for the privilege of having done it for His sake."* He simply applied Paul's advice: *"pray without ceasing." (1 Thess 5:17)* And, the spiritual giants of his day beat a path to his door.

One measure of the idolatrous potential of work is to ask about identity. When you meet a new neighbor or someone at a party, how does your spouse identify you? Is it by your marital relationship, by your favorite sport's team, or by your

---

1 This citation comes from the parable of the brats—one of my favorite (Matt 11:16–19).

profession?

What keeps you busy?

Loving Father. We praise you for giving us useful things to do. We praise for equipping us for work in your church. Thank you for giving us new eyes to see our work, our supervisors, and our primary responsibilities. The harvest is ready; prepare us to join the laborers. In the name of the Father, the Son, and the Holy Spirit, Amen.

Questions

1. How can work become an epicenter of idolatry? Why?
2. What does Jesus say about anxiety?
3. What brings dignity to our work?
4. Name two ways that the Apostle Paul transformed attitudes about work?
5. How can prayer be employed to transform our work?
6. How can work shape our personal identity?

DAY 45: *What is spiritual about marriage and family?*

"An excellent wife who can find? She is far more precious than jewels." (Prov 31:10)

*H*ow has marriage transformed you? If you are not married, how has your parent's marriage impacted you?

Scripture begins and ends with marriage. In Genesis, we see a couple, Adam and Eve, who are just made for each other! In the book of Revelation, an angel informs us: *"Blessed are those who are invited to the marriage supper of the Lamb." (Rev 19:9)* Obviously, marriage was God's idea (Keller 2011, 13).

As an unconditional promise—until death do us part, marriage is also formative and it provides a paradigm for other covenants. This implies that marriage, in and of itself, can function as a spiritual discipline.

The Apostle Paul's comments on mixed faith marriages highlight marriage's formative character. Paul reports that the believing spouse renders the whole marriage holy for the children (1 Cor 7:12–14). Paul also sees marriage as a witnessing opportunity. Paul asks: *"For how do you know, wife, whether you will save your husband? Or how do you know, husband, wheth-*

er you will save your wife?" (1 Cor 7:16)[1] In other words, Paul clearly sees marriage possessing a sacrificial component[2]. Jesus' own teaching on divorce and remarriage clearly draws inspiration, not from the Law of Moses (which admits exceptions), but rather from God's eternal work in creation[3].

But if marriage is a spiritual discipline, how does it draw us closer to God?

Marriage is formative in our faith for at least three reasons. The first reason is that God instituted marriage and commissioned marriage with a blessing and mandate: *"Be fruitful and multiply and fill the earth and subdue it, and have dominion . . ." (Gen 1:28)* God created marriage, blessed it, and said it was good—obeying God must draw us closer to him.

The second reason that marriage is formative is that it starts with an unconditional promise. God is the eternal promise keeper. In marriage we imitate our creator. Making and keeping good promises—even when it hurts—transforms us

---

1 A lot of ink has been spilt over the church's traditional teaching that forbid remarriage after divorce. For a discussion of the various perspectives, see: Wenham, Heth, and Keener (2006). My point is not to advocate a position but rather to recognize that marriage has a sacrificial component that often gets lost in our era of no-fault divorce.
2 In the Roman Catholic tradition, marriage is also a sacrament.
3 Deut 24: 1–4, Matt 19:6–9, and Gen 2:24.

and draws us closer to God.

The third reason marriage is formative is that it makes us accountable. Our spouses know us in the biblical (covenantal) way! Our weaknesses and sin affect our spouses and they tell us. We sin less, in part, because our spouses make us more aware of our sin—a sanctification process that forms us—even if we are not believers! Part of this process is to learn reconciliation skills by practicing them daily.[1] As the Apostle Paul wrote: *"And whatever you do, in word or deed, do everything in the name of the Lord Jesus, giving thanks to God the Father through him."* (Col 3:17)

This list of reasons why marriage is formative is especially interesting because God instituted marriage even before he instituted the nation of Israel or sent his son to die on the cross.

God is not irrational. He knows that the biggest beneficiaries of marriage are our children. And he loves them as much as he loves us. This is probably the reason that God places such

---

1 Marriage is so important in the Apostle Paul's thinking that he used the household codes (Eph 5:22–6:10; Col 3:17–4:4) as a metaphor for relationships in the church. Paul writes: *". . .if someone does not know how to manage his own household, how will he care for God's church?"* (1 Tim 3:5)

a high priority on marriage. We should too.

Almighty and loving God. We praise you for instituting and blessing our marriages. We thank you for the gift of children and for the way you transform us through and with our families. In the power of your Holy Spirit, grant us the wisdom and strength to care for our spouses and our children day by day. In Jesus' precious name, Amen.

Questions

1. Why should we believe that marriage was God's idea?

2. Why did the Apostle Paul believe that marriage is sacrificial?

3. What are three reasons why marriage should be considered a spiritual discipline?

4. Why does God place a high priority on marriage?

DAY 46: Why participate in a small group?

And day by day, attending the temple together and breaking bread in their homes, they received their food with glad and generous hearts, praising God and having favor with all the people. And the Lord added to their number day by day those who were being saved. (Acts 2:46–47)

*T*he early church was a small group. Many churches still are.

My first small group experience occurred in high school when our senior pastor retired and the youth director left. Overnight our active youth program fell apart. The associate pastor stepped in to fill the gap, but only two of us stuck with the group: my best friend and I. Throughout my senior year in high school, our time together focused on two things: the Book of Romans and Dietrich Bonhoeffer's book, *Cost of Discipleship.* Interestingly, my best friend and I are now both pastors.

The original small group is the Trinity—the Father, Son, and Holy Spirit. Because our identities are formed by who we are in relationship with[1], our relationship with the Triune God includes the example of what a loving, well-functioning com-

---

1 Maureen Miner (2007, 116) asks an important question: *"Can we have a separate and distinct relationship with each member of the Trinity?"* If so, striking the right balance requires a community effort which is a mandate for small groups.

munity looks like[2].

Another foundational small group is the family. Families talk about every important matter in life. In the family, we learn to talk, pray, and to read scripture. Our families also teach us to joke, to love, to fight, and to reconcile. My first ministry as an adult was to my family.

Jesus did not write a book; he established a small group. This simple observation is remarkable because Jesus drew large crowds—therefore, his focus on disciplining the twelve appeared counter-intuitive. Jesus called the twelve disciples after spending an entire night in prayer (Luke 6:12). The Gospels record how very difficult the journey of faith was for Jesus' disciples. Not all of them made it (John 6:66).

Small groups provide us the security to make difficult transitions (Icenogle 1994, 126–37)[3]. Most tragedies in life are involuntary transitions. During such transitions, we often cry: Lord—why me? Transitions become growth opportunities

---

2 This relationship has a name: perichoresis, which means divine dance. It defines the special and intimate relationship we see in the Trinity (Keller 2008, 213–26).

3 Consultant William Bridges (2003, 43) makes the point that it took Moses maybe 40 days to get the people of Israel out of Egypt, but it took about 40 years to get the Egypt out of the people (Num 11:5). The point is that transitions begin with people looking backwards; proceed through a long period of uncertainty; and end as people began to adapt to the new environment (Bridges 2003, 100). After 40 years in the wilderness, it took new leadership, Joshua, to lead the people of Israel into the Promised Land.

when we pray: Lord—why did you bring me to this time and place? Small groups provide a safe place to ask this question while inviting members to wait upon the Lord's response together.

Holy Father. We praise you for your divine example of life in community. Shelter us through life's transitions. Grant us spiritual guides for the journey who help us ask the right questions and persevere with us until we do. In the power of your Holy Spirit, teach us to accept guidance and how to offer it in grace. In Jesus' name, Amen.

Questions

1. What small group activities defined the early church?

2. Are numbers always a measure of small group success?

3. What was the original small group?

4. What is a transition?

5. What spiritual question can be posed effectively in a transition?

DAY 47: Why Sabbath rest?

"the Son of Man is lord of the Sabbath." (Matt 12:8)

What is the first sin in the Bible?

The typical response is that the first sin occurred when Adam and Eve ate from the tree of the knowledge of good and evil (Gen 3:6). An alternative interpretation points out that although Adam and Eve were created in Genesis 1, when God rests on the first Sabbath in Genesis 2 they are not mentioned (Feinberg 1998, 16). The first sin in scripture is then argued to be a sin of omission (not doing good)—of Adam and Eve refusing to participate in Sabbath rest. It was as if God threw a party and they refused to come[1].

After that, the sin in Genesis escalated from disrespect into open rebellion. In Genesis 3, Adam and Eve commit their first sin of commission (doing evil). In Genesis 4, Cain kills Abel and Lamech takes revenge. In Genesis 5, Noah—the man who rested—is born[2]. In Genesis 6, God tells Noah to build an ark because he planned to send a flood in response to the depth of human corruption and sin. After the flood, only Noah and

---

[1] One weakness with this interpretation is that Adam and Eve felt guilty over their nakedness, not other things such as empathy over the pain that they caused God (Gen 3:7).

[2] In Hebrew, Noah means he rests (Feinberg 1998, 28). Also see: Kline (2006, 229).

his family remained[1].

This interpretation is echoed in the New Testament where the kingdom of God compared to a wedding. Jesus tells an enigmatic parable of a king who held a wedding banquet for his son. When the banquet was ready, the king sent his servants to inform his guests. But, instead of responding to the reminder, many of the intended guests ignored the invitation while others committed acts of violence, even murder, against the king's servants. The climax to this story comes in verse 7: *"The king was angry, and he sent his troops and destroyed those murderers and burned their city." (Matt 22:7)*

If we treat Sabbath rest as a foretaste of the kingdom of God, this parable can be an allegory to the first sin, in which Adam and Eve refused God's invitation to join him in the first Sabbath. The original sin, according to this interpretation, was the contemptuous rejection of God's generous invitation on the seventh day. The fact that the parable of the wedding feast is a parable of judgment is an emphatic reminder that GOD REALLY WANTS US TO REST WITH HIM.

Sabbath rest is important enough to God that is the fourth and the longest of the Ten Commandments given to Mo-

1 Kline (2006, 221–27) views story of Noah as a re-creation event. Noah's ark serves as a prototype of the tabernacle, the temple, and, ultimately, heaven itself.

ses (Exod 20:8–11). Why was it important to the Jewish people? Free people rest; slaves work. The experience of slavery in Egypt and later in Babylon was a reminder that rest is a privilege not always enjoyed.

Are we a free people? Do we rest? Do we rest with God?

Jesus described himself as the Lord of the Sabbath, not to do away with it, but to refocus it on God's desire for our lives. Sabbath rest is a gateway to the other spiritual disciplines because it makes the other disciplines easier to pursue. Rested people have the energy to care. Exhausted people struggle to care for God and for their neighbors.

Confusion about Sabbath arises, in part, because the Jewish Sabbath was the last day of the week, while Christians celebrated Sabbath on the first day of the week[2]. Pastors and others that must work Sundays often designate another day as their Sabbath and inform their family and friends. The point is to consecrate a day each week to honor and rest with God.

Gracious Father. Rest with us. Grant us the energy to care. Let us focus a day each week on being your people and modeling

---

2 Chang (2006, 81) writes: *"Sunday is the first day of the week, but the early Christians also called it the eighth day. By call it the eighth day, the Christian understood the resurrection event as breaking through the earthly limitation of the weekly cycle."*

your love to those around us. In the name of the Father, the Son, and the Holy Spirit, Amen.

Questions

1.   What was the first sin in scripture?

2.   What is the difference between a sin of omission and one of commission?

3.   What is an allegory?

4.   Why is Sabbath rest important in Jewish history? Why is it important to God?

5.   How is Sabbath rest a gateway to the spiritual disciplines?

DAY 48: What is worship?

. . . the twenty-four elders fall down before him who is seated on the throne and worship him who lives forever and ever. They cast their crowns before the throne, saying, Worthy are you, our Lord and God, to receive glory and honor and power, for you created all things, and by your will they existed and were created. (Rev 4:10–11)

*I*f a spiritual discipline points us to God, then worship is the prince of the spiritual disciplines. In fact, we were made for worship (Calhoun 2005, 25).

Unfortunately, the Bible's first picture of worship also pictures improper worship. Cain brought God some fruit; Abel slaughtered the first born of his flock and brought God the fat portions. God honored Abel's sacrifice, but not Cain's (Gen 4:3–5). Improper worship is like inviting your supervisor to your house and serving leftovers at dinner—you may not get fired, but it degrades the relationship.

One of the first deacons of the church, Stephen, was arrested in Jerusalem and was arraigned before the Sanhedrin. There, he accused them of limiting the access to God at the temple, of killing the prophets, of betraying and murdering Christ, and, therefore, of not keeping the law. Improper worship—limiting access to God—was Stephen's first charge. For this and other things, they took Stephen out and stoned him (Acts 7:48–58).

Stephen's complaint was not about altar sacrifices. When the Israelite people lived in Egypt, they needed to go into the wilderness to offer sacrifices, in part, because they sacrificed animals that were sacred to the Egyptians (Exod 8:26). The point of the sacrifice was to demonstrate loyalty to God by forsaking the typical idols of the day (Lev 17:7)[1]. However, over time the sacrifices lost their meaning, became routine, or, worse, started to look like divine bribes—improper worship[2]. Echoing the Prophet Isaiah (1:16), King David writes: *"The sacrifices of God are a broken spirit; a broken and contrite heart, O God, you will not despise."* *(Ps 51:17)* The content of worship, not its form, is what makes worship proper or improver.

An important picture of proper worship is given in Revelation 4:10–11 where the twenty-four elders cast their crowns before the throne of God. In heaven, the elders are casting down crowns given them by God, yet they still humbly lay them

---

1 For more discussion, see: (Hahn 2009, 150).

2 For example, the Prophet Isaiah (1:13) writes: *"bring no more vain offerings; incense is an abomination to me. New moon and Sabbath and the calling of convocations—I cannot endure iniquity and solemn assembly."* Likewise, the prophet Malachi writes: *"When you offer blind animals in sacrifice, is that not evil?"* *(Mal 1:8)*

down (e.g. Rev 2:10). On earth, a crown is a symbol (an idol) of our vanity—a conspicuous display of personal wealth, power, and authority; it does not have to be a golden tiara! When I cast my crowns at the feet of the king of kings, I am surrendering all my idols—money, power, and authority—to God. *On earth as it is in heaven* this is the ultimate act of worship.

How do we then properly lay our crowns before the Lord?

Proper worship is an idol crashing event[3]. In worship we demonstrate our loyalty to God by surrendering to God the idols that most typically capture our hearts—our money, our power, and our authority. For some, it will mean writing checks; for others it may be donating time; for still others it may be simply to show up at worship clean and sober. For most of us, it means bringing along our families. For all of us, it means joining in God's praises. Worship is a smorgasbord of praise.

When we look beyond our pride and idols to God, we

---

3 The prophet Mohammed (1934, 21.51–.66) wrote that Abraham's father was an idol-maker. One day when his father was away, Abraham smashed all but the biggest idol in his shop. When his father returned and confronted him, Abraham told his father to ask the remaining idol what happened. His father replied—you know that idols cannot speak. To which Abraham responded—then why do you worship anything but the living God?

cast down our crowns and truly worship.

Almighty Father. We praise you for who you and for being worthy of our praise. Draw us to yourself. Reconcile us with our neighbors. May we lay our crowns before you and rest only with you. In the power of your Holy Spirit, open our hearts; illumine our minds; strengthen our hands in your service. In the Jesus' name, Amen.

Questions

1.	Why should worship be called the prince of the spiritual disciplines?

2.	What are some biblical examples of improper worship?

3.	What does it mean to cast our crowns before the throne of God?

4.	In what way is worship sacrificial? What does worship have to do with smashing idols?

CONCLUSIONS

WHAT ARE THE BIG QUESTIONS OF THE FAITH?

HOW DO WE NURTURE OUR WALK WITH THE LORD?

DAY 49: *What are the big questions of the faith?*

"For God so loved the world, that he gave his only Son, that whoever believes in him should not perish but have eternal life." (John 3:16)

How does the Christian answer the four big questions of faith?[1] The Apostle's Creed, the Lord's Prayer, and the Ten Commandments offer real insights.

WHO IS GOD? In the Apostle's Creed, God is one God in three persons—Father, Son, and Holy Spirit—who we can know through the story of Jesus as revealed in scripture. In the Lord's Prayer, God, through His sovereign rule over all creation, shapes us in his image day by day as we walk in obedience to Him. In the Ten Commandments, God is the supreme covenant maker who expresses his love for us through concrete guidance. The Triune God is alive and works in the world to form the church, forgive sin, and grant us re-created life.

WHO ARE WE? In the Apostle's Creed, we are invited into relationship with the Triune God and to participate in the story of Jesus. In the Lord's Prayer, we are seen as created in God's image which then offers us dignity and intrinsic value.

---

1 As mentioned earlier, the four big questions in philosophy are: metaphysics (Who is God?), epistemology (How do we know?), and anthropology (Who are we?), and ethics (What is good to do?) (Kreeft 2007, 6).

However, our reflection of God's image is imperfect because of the influence of sin. In the Ten Commandments, God initiates a covenant relationship with us, which provides us clear guidance for living in a way that pleases Him.

WHAT IS GOOD TO DO? In the Apostle's Creed, a detailed picture of God is presented, especially in the life and work of Jesus Christ, in whom we are exhorted to believe and emulate in life, death, and resurrection (Phil 3:9–11). In the Lord's Prayer, we are enabled to commune directly with God in prayer and in bearing God's image in the world. In the Ten Commandments, law guides us in daily living through concrete action.

HOW DO WE KNOW? The Apostle's Creed reminds us that we stand together with the church throughout the ages before a holy and loving God. Scripture records the Ten Commandments and the Lord's Prayer. The Holy Spirit inspired the authors and illuminates our reading. Christ's divinity anchors scripture because Jesus expressed confidence in it (Matt 5:18). As Jesus prophesied—*"if these were silent, the very stones would cry out"*—archeological research has confirmed the validity of many events and places in scripture (Luke 19:40)[2].

Our faith in God is paradoxical[3]. Like the child who is

2 If you are unconvinced, read a few of the stories in the *NIV Archaeological Study Bible* (Zondervan, 2005).

3 The Apostle Paul wrote: *"For he was crucified in weakness, but lives by the*

able to play with abandon because of the watchful eye of a parent, we are free in Christ to live within God's will for our lives. In Christ, the gap of time, space, and holiness between us and God is bridged. Freedom in Christ accordingly brings rest for our souls[1].

Heavenly Father, beloved Son, Holy Spirit. We thank you that you do not leave us alone and that you care for us. Inspire our hearts and illumine our minds so that we can be light in a dark and confusing world. In Jesus' precious name, Amen.

Questions

1. What are the four big questions of faith?

2. How do the Ten Commandments, the Lord's Prayer, and the Apostle's Creed help us understand these questions?

3. In your own words, how would you answer these questions?

---

power of God. For we also are weak in him, but in dealing with you we will live with him by the power of God." (2 Cor 13:4).

1 Jesus said: "Take my yoke upon you, and learn from me, for I am gentle and lowly in heart, and you will find rest for your souls." (Matt 11:29)

DAY 50: *How do we nurture our walk with the Lord?*

*Put on then, as God's chosen ones, holy and beloved, compassion-
ate hearts, kindness, humility, meekness, and patience, bearing
with one another and, if one has a complaint against another,
forgiving each other; as the Lord has forgiven you, so you also
must forgive. (Col 3:12–13)*

We must nurture our walk with the Lord, but control is not in our hands. *"Discipleship means adherence to Christ"* (Bonhoeffer 1995, 59).

Jesus tells the story of a man with two sons. The younger son came to him one day and asked for his inheritance in cash. He then took the money, left town, and began living in style. This reckless lifestyle did not last long and soon the young man had to get a job. Not being a planner, he had to accept degrading work. As the son's mind began to wander, he remembered his good life at home and resolved to beg his father to take him back as a household servant. When the father saw that his son was coming, he went out to meet him and wrapped his arms around him. As the son began to apologize for his horrible behavior, his father would hear none of it. He took his son; cleaned him up; got him some new clothes[1]; and threw a party.

1 As Christians, we share mostly just one thing in common: we are forgiven. It is our heavenly Father who clothes us with: *"compassionate hearts, kind-*

Later, when his older brother came home and discovered the party, he became jealous and started behaving badly. But his father reminded him: *"celebrate and be glad, for this your brother was dead, and is alive; he was lost, and is found."* *(Luke 15:32)*

The story of the Prodigal Son shows a young man going through a series of challenges—transitions—that enabled him to see his father with new eyes and to accept his father's help[1]. Without these challenges, he would not have been able to bridge the gap between him and his father.

For us, hospital visits often pose such transitions. Hospital visits normally start with a health problem; lead to a confusing period of medical treatment; and end with a return to life outside. The twist is that the health problem itself is often a symptom, not the real cause, of the visit. The real problem may be grief over the death of a family member, unresolved trauma from the past, or a bad lifestyle choice. Because a solution to the real problem remains clouded by denial, many people needlessly die of preventable diseases and treatable ailments.

Clouds also cover our journey of faith. We all deny the need for God's grace and have nasty stumbling blocks—espe-

---

ness, humility, meekness, and patience." *(Col 3:12)* But the clothes are a gift, we did not earn them!

1 Turansky and Miller (2013,4) observe: *"Even in Old Testament times, God knew that kids learn best through life experiences."*

cially pride, other sins, and our own mortality—that must be removed in order to deliver us from our focus on ourselves. It is only through accepting God's grace that we are able to take the necessary steps of obedience.

The story of the Prodigal Son assures us that our heavenly Father is anxious to forgive, anxious for us to take steps of obedience, and anxious to bridge the gap that we cannot bridge ourselves.

Loving Father. Thank you for forgiving us and accepting us back as sons and daughters. Grant us teachable hearts, discerning minds, and strength for each new day. In the power of your Holy Spirit, reveal to us the stumbling blocks that impede our progress as faithful servants. In Jesus precious name, Amen.

Questions

1.   Who owns our spiritual walk and who is in control?

2.   What is the faith lesson in the story of the young son?

3.   What does everyone in the church share in common?

4.   What is a stumbling block in faith? Are they obvious to us? How do we learn about our own stumbling blocks?

5.   How is a hospital visit a transition? How does it relate to

our journey of faith?

REFERENCES

Aquinas, Thomas. 2003. *On Evil (Orig Pub 1270)*. Translated by Richard Regan. Edited by Brian Davies. New York: Oxford University Press.

Alcorn, Randy. 2006. *50 Days in Heaven: Reflections that Bring Eternity to Life*. Carol Stream, IL: Tyndale House Publishers, Inc.

Arendt, Hannah. 1992. *Lectures on Kant's Political Philosophy*. Chicago: University of Chicago Press.

Bainton, Roland H. 1995. *Here I Stand: A Life of Martin Luther*. New York: Penguin.

Bauer, Walter (BDAG). 2000. *A Greek-English Lexicon of the New Testament and Other Early Christian Literature*. 3rd ed. Ed. Frederick W. Danker. Chicago: University of Chicago Press. <BibleWorks. v.9.>.

Benner, David G. 2203. *Sacred Companions: The Gift of Spiritual Friendship & Direction*. Downers Grove, IL: IVP Books.

BibleWorks. 2011. *Norfolk, VA: BibleWorks, LLC*. <BibleWorks v.9>.

Billings, J. Todd. 2009. *Calvin, Participation and the Gift: The Activity of Believers in Union with Christ*. New York: Oxford University Press.

Bonhoeffer, Dietrich. 1995. *The Cost of Discipleship (Orig.* pub. 1937). New York: Simon and Schuster.

Bridges, Jerry. 1996. *The Pursuit of Holiness*. Colorado Springs: NavPress.

Bridges, William. 2003. *Managing Transitions: Making the Most of Change*. Cambridge, MA: Da Capo Press.

Calhoun, Adele Ahlberg. 2005. *Spiritual Disciplines Handbook: Practices that Transform Us*. Downers Grove, IL: IVP Books.

Calvin, John. 2006. *Institutes of the Christian Religion (Orig Pub 1559)*. Edited by John T. McNeill. Translated by Ford Lewis Battles. Louisville, KY: Westminster John Knox Press.

Card, Michael. 2005. *A Sacred Sorrow: Reaching Out to God in the Lost Language of Lament*. Colorado Springs: NavPress.

Chan, Simon. 1998. *Spiritual Theology: A Systemic Study of the Christian Life*. Downers Grove, IL: IVP Academic.

Chan, Simon. 2006. *Liturgical Theology: The Church as a Worshiping Community*. Downers Grove, IL: IVP Academic.

Cloud, Henry. 2008. *The One-Life Solution: Reclaim Your Personal Life While Achieving Greater Personal Success*. New York: Harper.

Dyck, Drew Nathan. 2014. *Yawning at Tigers: You Can't Tame God, So Stop Trying*. Nashville: Thomas Nelson.

Dyrness, William A. 2001. *Visual Faith: Art, Theology, and Worship in Dialogue*. Grand Rapids, MI: Baker Academic.

Elliott, Matthew A. 2006. *Faithful Feelings: Rethinking Emotion in the New Testament*. Grand Rapids, MI: Kregel.

Evans, Craig A. 2005. *Ancient Texts for New Testament Studies: A Guide to Background Literature*. Peabody, MA: Hendrickson.

Fairlie, Henry. 2006. *The Seven Deadly Sins Today (Orig Pub 1978)*. Notre Dame, IN: University of Notre Dame Press.

Faith Alive Christian Resources (FACR). 2013. *The Heidelberg Catechism*. Cited: 30 August, 2013. Online: https://www.rca.org/sslpage.aspx?pid=372.

Feinberg, Jeffrey Enoch. 1998. *Walk Genesis: A Messianic Jewish Devotional Commentary*. Clarksville, MD: Lederer Books.

Foster, Richard J., 1992. *Prayer: Find the Heat's True Home*. New York: HarperOne.

Fox, John and Harold J. Chadwick. 2001. *The New Foxes' Book of Martyrs (Orig Pub 1563)*. Gainsville, FL: Bridge-Logos Publishers.

Giglio, Louie. 2003. *The Air I Breathe*. Colorado Springs: Multnomah Press.

Hahn, Scott W. 2009. *Kinship by Covenant: A Canonical Approach to the Fulfillment of God's Saving Promises*. New Haven, CT: Yale University Press.

Haas, Guenther H. 2004. *"Calvin's Ethics."* In The Cambridge Companion to John Calvin, 93–105. Edited by Donald K. McKim. New York: Cambridge University Press.

Hudson, Robert [Editor]. 2004. *Christian Writers Manual on Style*. Grand Rapids, MI: Zondervan.

Hugenberger, Gordon P. 1994. *Marriage as a Covenant: Biblical Law and Ethics as Developed from Malachi*. Grand Rapids, MI: Baker Academic.

Hugenberger, Gordon P. 1994. *The Lord's Prayer: A Guide for the Perplexed*. Boston: Park Street Church.

Icenogle, Gareth Weldon. 1994. *Biblical Foundations for Small Group Ministry: An Integrational Approach*. Downers Grove, IL: InterVarsity Press.

Josephus, Flavius. 2009. *The Antiquities of the Jews*. Translated by William Whiston. Cited: 30 August 2013. Online: http://www.gutenberg.org/ebooks/2848.

Keller, Timothy. 2008. *The Reason for God: Belief in an Age of Skepticism*. New York: Dutton.

Keller, Timothy and Kathy Keller. 2011. *The Meaning of Marriage: Facing the Complexities of Commitment with the Wisdom of God*. New York: Dutton.

Kline, Meredith G. 1963. *Treaty of the Great King: The Covenantal Structure of Deteronomy—Studies and Commentary*. Eugene, OR: Wipf & Stock Publishers.

Kline, Meredith G. 2006. *Kingdom Prologue: Genesis Foundations for a Convenental Worldview*. Eugene, OR: Wipf & Stock Publishers.

Kreeft, Peter. 2007. *The Philosophy of Jesus*. South Bend, IN: Saint Augustine's Press.

Lawrence, Brother. 1982. *The Practice of the Presence of God (Orig Pub 1691)*. New Kensington, PA: Whitaker House.

Lewis, C. S. 1973. T*he Great Divorce: A Dream (Orig Pub 1946)*. New York: HarperOne.

Lewis, C. S. 2001. *Mere Christianity* (Orig Pub 1950). New York: Harper Collins Publishers, Inc.

Macchia, Stephen A. 2012. *Crafting a Rule of Life: An Invitation to the Well-Ordered Way*. Downers Grove: IVP Books.

May, Gerald G. 1988. *Addiction and Grace: Love and Spirituality in the Healing of Addictions*. New York: HarperOne.

Metaxas, Eric. 2010. *Bonhoeffer: Pastor, Martyr, Prophet, Spy—A Righteous Gentile Versus The Third Reich*. Nashville: Thomas Nelson.

Metzger, Bruce M. and Bart D. Ehrman. 2005. *The Text of the New Testament: Its Transmission, Corruption, and Restoration*. New York: Oxford University Press.

Neder, Adam. 2009. *Participation in Christ: An Entry into Karl Barth's Church Dogmatics*. Louisville: Westminster John Knox Press.

Niehaus, Jeffery. 2010. *"Covenant and Narrative, God and Time."* Journal of the Evangelical Theological Society. 53:3, 535–59.

Nouwen, Henri J. M. 1975. *Reaching Out: The Three Movements of the Spiritual Life*. New York: DoubleDay.

Nouwen, Henri J. M. 2002. *In the Name of Jesus: Reflections on Christian Leadership*. New York: Crossroad Publishing Company.

MacNutt, Francis. 2009. *Healing*. Notre Dame, IN: Ave Maria Press.

Miner, Maureen. 2007. *"Back to the basics in attachment to God: Revisiting theory in light of theology."* Journal of Psychology and Theology, 35(2), 112–22.

Mohammed. 1934. *The Holy Qur'an: Text Translation, and Commentary*. Translated by A.Yusuf Ali. Washington DC: The Islamic Center.

Presbyterian Church in the United States of America (PC USA). 1999. *The Constitution of the Presbyterian Church (U.S.A.)*—Part I: Book of Confession. Louisville, KY: Office of the General Assembly.

Reynolds, Steve and MG Ellis. 2012. *Get Off the Couch: 6 Motivators to Help You Lose Weight and Start Living*. Ventura: Regal.

Rice, Howard L. 1991. *Reformed Spirituality: An Introduction for Believers*. Louisville: Westminster John Knox Press.

Rogers, Jack. 1991. *Presbyterian Creeds: A Guide to the Book of Confessions*. Louisville, KY: Westminster John Knox Press.

Rosen, Sidney [Editor]. 1982. *My Voice will Go With You: The Teaching Tales of Milton H. Erickson*. New York: W.W. Norton and Company.

Sande, Ken. 2004. *The Peace Maker: A Biblical Guide to Resolving Personal Conflict*. Grand Rapids, MI: BakerBooks.

Smith, Houston. 2001. *Why Religion Matters: The Fate of the Human Spirit in an Age of Disbelief*. San Francisco: Harper.

Sproul, R.C. 2003. *Defending Your Faith: An Introduction to Apologetics*. Wheaton, IL: Crossway Books.

Stasssen, Glen H. and David P. Gushee. 2003. *Kingdom Ethics: Following Jesus in Contemporary Context*. Downers Grove, IL: IVP Academic.

Stone, Larry. 2010. *The Story of the Bible: The Fascinating History of Its Writing, Translation, and Effect on Civilization*. Nashville, TN: Thomas Nelson.

Thielicke, Helmut. 1962. *A Little Exercise for Young Theologians*. Grand Rapids, MI: Eerdmans.

Thomas, Gary. 2010. *Sacred Pathways: Discover Your Soul's Path to God*. Grand Rapids, MI: Zondervan.

Trueblood, Eldon. 1964. *The Humor of Christ*. New York: Harper & Row, Publishers.

Turansky, Scott and Joanne Miller. 2013. *The Christian Parenting Handbook: 50 Heart-Based Strategies for All the Stages of Your Child's Life*. Nashville: Thomas Nelson.

U.S. Census Bureau. 2011. *Statistical Abstract of the United States: 2011*. Washington, DC: Government Printing Office.

Wenham, Gordon J., William A. Heth, and Craig S. Keener. 2006. *Remarriage After Divorce in Today's Church: Three Views*. Grand Rapids, MI: Zondervan.

Whelchel, Hugh. 2012. *How Then Should We Work? Rediscovering the Biblical Doctrine of Work*. Bloomington, IN: WestBow Press.

Wilberforce, William. 2006. *A Practical View of Christianity (Orig.* pub. 1797). Ed. Kevin Charles Belmonte. Peabody, MA: Hendrickson Christian Classics; Hendrickson Publishers.

Zondervan. 2005. *NIV Archaeological Study Bible: An Illustrated Walk Through Biblical History and Culture*. Grand Rapids, MI: Zondervan.

SCRIPTURAL INDEX

ABOUT THE AUTHOR

*A*uthor Stephen W. Hiemstra (MDiv, PhD) is a slave of Christ, husband, father, tentmaker, economist, and writer. He lives with Maryam, his wife of thirty years, in Centreville, VA and they have three grown children.

Stephen has been an active writer throughout his career; both as an economist, and as a pastor. As an economist of 27 years in 5 federal agencies, he published numerous government studies, magazine articles, and book reviews. *A Christian Guide to Spirituality* is, however, his first published book[1].

Stephen is currently a second career tentmaker dividing his time equally between Hispanic ministry and blogging with an *online pastor* theme—this online ministry normally takes the form of offering bible studies, writing commentaries on helpful books, and reflecting on spiritual topics. As a hospital chaplain intern, he worked in the emergency department, a psychiatric unit, and an Alzheimer's unit. He is an elder in Centreville Presbyterian Church.

He has a masters of divinity (MDiv, 2013) from Gordon-Conwell Theological Seminary in Charlotte, NC. His doctorate (PhD, 1985) is in agricultural economics from Michigan

---

1 A *Leader Guide* and *Media Guide* are available online at T2Pneuma.com.

State University in East Lansing, MI. Although a U.S. citizen, Stephen lived and studied both in Puerto Rico and Germany, and is conversational in both Spanish and German.

Please correspond with Stephen at: T2Pneuma@gmail.com or follow him on social media[2].

---

2 Stephen is most active in blogging (T2Pneuma.net) and Tweeting (@ T2Pneuma).

Made in the USA
Charleston, SC
15 August 2014